True Self

True Self

How To Reconnect With Your True Self

Oliver JR Cooper

Also By Oliver JR Cooper

Books

A Dialogue With The Heart – Part One: A Collection Of Poems And Dialogues From The Heart

Trapped Emotions – How Are They Affecting Your Life

Childhood – Is Your Childhood Sabotaging Your Life?

A Dialogue With The Heart – Part Two: A Collection Of Poems And Dialogues From The Heart

Toxic Shame – Is It Defining Your Life?

Abandonment – Is The Fear Of Abandonment Controlling Your Life?

Child Abuse – Were You Abused As A Child?

A Dialogue With The Spirit – A Collection Of Poems And Dialogues To Help You Grieve The Loss Of A Loved One

Trapped Grief – Is Trapped Grief Sabotaging Your Life?

Why Does He Behave That Way? Why Do I Behave This Way?

Boundaries – Are You Boundaryless?

Inner Child – Is Your Inner Child Controlling Your Life? **(Also available as an audiobook)**

Childhood Trauma – Is Childhood Trauma Defining Your Life?

People Pleasing – Is Your Need To Please Others Sabotaging Your Life?

Loyalty – Is Your Need To Be Loyal Sabotaging Your Life?

Trauma – Is Trauma Sabotaging Your Life?

How-To Guides

Inner Child – How To Heal Your Inner Child

Self-Awareness – How To Develop Self-Awareness

Purpose – How To Find Your Purpose

Anxiety – How To Deal With Your Anxiety

Breakups – How To Get Over A Breakup

Fear Of Abandonment – How To Heal Your Fear Of Abandonment

Self-Love – How To Develop Self-Love And Self-Worth

Child Abuse And Neglect – How To Heal From Child Abuse And Neglect

Mother-Enmeshed Man – How To No longer Be A Mother-Enmeshed Man

Note to Readers

That which is contained within this book is based upon my own experiences, research and views up until the point of publication. It is not to be taken as the truth or the only viable viewpoint. It is not intended to diagnose or cure any disease.

This book is dedicated to Adam Jordan. Thank you for being there for me.

True Self – How To Reconnect With Your True Self

© 2023 Oliver JR Cooper

ISBN: 9798391872375

For information, please contact:

www.oliverjrcooper.co.uk

Contents

Introduction 1

The First Part - Examples Of The False Self

Chapter 1: Assertiveness – Do You Find It
Hard To Assert Yourself? 15

Chapter 2: Being Seen – Do You Hide? 19

Chapter 3: Boundaries – Do You Lack
Boundaries? 23

Chapter 4: Confidence – Do You Only Feel
Confident When You Play A Role? 29

Chapter 5: People Pleasing – Do You Try To
Please Others?.. 33

Chapter 6: Relationships – Do You Always
Act Like You Have It All Together? 37

Chapter 7: Relationships – Do You Neglect
Your   Own Needs When You Are In A
Relationship?.. 41

Chapter 8: Relationships – Do You Play A
Role?.. 45

Chapter 9: Relationships – Do You Try To
Fix Others?... 51

Chapter 10: Relationships – Do You Try To
Rescue Others?... 55

Chapter 11: Self-Care – Do You Find It Hard
To   Relax?.. 59

Chapter 12: Self-Expression – Do You Hide How You Feel?.. 65

Chapter 13: Self-Worth – Do You Believe That You Need To Be Good At Everything? 71

Chapter 14: Self-Worth – Do You Only Feel Valuable When You Please Others? 77

Chapter 15: Self-Worth – Do You Believe That Your Value Is Defined By What You Do?........................... 81

Chapter 16: Sense Of Self – Do You Feel Empty? 85

Chapter 17: Success – Are You An Overachiever? ... 91

The Second Part - How To Reconnect To Your True-Self

Chapter 18: The Power Of Letting Go 99

Chapter 19: A Unique Path....................................... 103

Chapter 20: The Body And The Mind 105

Chapter 21: The First Step 113

Chapter 22: The Second Step 117

Chapter 23: The Third Step 131

Chapter 24: The Importance Of Touch 137

Chapter 25: Journaling, Creativity, And Travel 139

Chapter 26: Self-Activation 143

Chapter 27: Two Common Sayings 145

Chapter 28: What Did You Lose? 147

Chapter 29: Inner Conflict.. 149

Chapter 30: Unhealthy Guilt 151

Chapter 31: Forgiveness 153

Chapter 32: Supportive Relationships 159

Chapter 33: The Power Of Visualisation 161

Chapter 34: The Power Of Your Environment 165

Chapter 35: Are You Following Your Calling?.......... 169

Chapter 36: Energy 173

Chapter 37: The Power Of Your Attention 177

Chapter 38: Emotional Awareness 181

Chapter 39: A Useful System 183

Afterword.. 185

Acknowledgements 189

Introduction

To some, the term 'true self' can sound a bit airy-fairy and something that has very little, if any, basis in reality. This can then be seen as something that someone would believe if they were 'spiritual' and had their head in the clouds.

They could point out that a human being is not like a statue that doesn't change; they are constantly changing. So, to say that there is a false self or a true self is going to be nothing more than an illusion.

However, while some people will respond in this manner, it doesn't mean that they have an accurate idea of what is meant by these terms. In reality, there is nothing about these terms that has anything to do with an illusion.

Then again, that would be inaccurate as the false self is not real in the sense that it relates to something substantial and has firm foundations. This relates to a disconnected self that is outer-directed, as opposed to inner-directed, and, thus, relates to the ways in which someone can behave that have very little to do with their true essence.

Their true self, on the other hand, relates to them being connected to their body (this is why, if someone is not connected to their body, they can see themselves as a nobody) and in tune with their true needs, feelings, wants, preferences and longings. Therefore, when someone pays attention to this information and allows this information to guide them, they will be behaving in an authentic manner.

However, this embodied self won't be purely inner-directed, as someone who is in this position will also be aware of and influenced by what is going on externally. But, by being balanced and not being overly focused on what is going on externally, they will be able to live a fulfilling life.

Another part of this is that by having this connection to themselves, they will be able to take life in, give and receive love, and experience deeper connections with others. Their connection to themselves and being able to feel will allow them to embrace life and those with who they choose to get close (it has been said that to the degree that someone can embrace their own body is the degree that they will be able to embrace life. How deeply they generally breathe has also been said to reveal the same thing).

There are going to be some people on this planet who have more or less always experienced life in this way, and then there are going to be plenty of others who experience life differently. But even if someone does experience life in this way, it doesn't mean that they will realise they are in touch with their true self.

The reason for this is that if this is how their life has been for a long time, it can just be what is normal. They will reap the benefits of having this connection with themselves, but they may not necessarily know that it is because they are in tune with themselves.

And the same could be said for someone who is out of touch with themselves, as they might not even realise this either. Their life is unlikely to be very fulfilling, but that doesn't mean that they will say to themselves, "My life would be different if I let go of my false self."

It has been argued that the only way that someone can find out what the false self is, is by finding out what it isn't. This is clearly a good way to start, especially if someone is not even aware that they are out of touch with themselves.

Still, while this is a process that will be important for anyone who is not living a fulfilling life, it is often something that begins after someone has hit rock bottom. They will then have reached a point where they can no longer take any more, causing them to come to the conclusion that enough is well and truly enough.

At this stage in their life, wearing a mask is no longer going to benefit them like it used to. The pay-off that they used to get through ignoring themselves is no longer going to cut it.

This could mean that they are at the beginning of their life, or they could be at another stage of it. Yet, regardless of how long they have been on this planet, the time will have come for them to embrace their true nature.

When it comes to whether or not someone is in touch with who they are, what is likely to play the biggest part is what their developmental years were like. This time in their life would then have defined if they were able to stay connected to who they are, assuming that they were not born in a disconnected state, and then to develop a stronger connection as time went by, or if they had to disconnect from themselves and create an unreal self.

What this shows is that someone doesn't just come into the world with a fully developed self. No, this is something that occurs through receiving the right attunement and care from the moment they are born.

If the right attunement and care are generally provided, there is a strong chance that someone will be able to develop in the right way and go through each developmental stage (look into Erik Erikson's 8 stages of development for more details). Not only will they stay connected to their inner world, but they will feel as though it is safe for them to allow their inner world to have an effect on how they behave.

Their parent or parents' will show them that it is safe for them to exist and to be who they are and that who they are (and this will include their needs and feelings) is worthy, enough, and lovable, and this will allow them to develop a felt sense of safety, trust, belonging, worthiness, enoughness, lovability and give them the strength that they need to be themselves when the time comes for them to go out into the real world and stand on their own two feet (to go from what is often described as the unconditional world to the world that is largely conditional). Said another way, it will cause them to develop both the being and the doing side of their nature (the feminine and masculine).

This could be seen as the main job that a parent has – to give a child what they need so that they can handle life by themselves. Unfortunately, this is not something that always takes place, which is one of the main reasons why the world is the way it is.

When this doesn't happen, a child won't be able to receive what they need to develop in the right way. Instead of receiving the right nutrients, so to speak, a child will end up being undermined.

This will be a time when their brain and nervous system are not equipped to handle a lot of stress, yet that is exactly what they will experience. The kind of experiences that they will have during this time can be hard for an adult to handle, let alone a child.

This can be a time when they will be abused and/or neglected and deprived of what they need. The love that they need to grow won't be provided (to put it another way, a number of their developmental needs won't be met on a consistent basis) and this will cause them to stay in an underdeveloped state and develop a felt sense that it is not safe enough for them to exist, that others can't be trusted to be there for them, that they don't belong, that there is something inherently wrong with them and their needs and feelings, that they are not enough and that they are unlovable.

Said another way, it will cause them to develop an over-developed doing side and end up with an under-developed being side (a strong masculine element and a weak feminine element). They won't be able to see that how they are being treated isn't personal and is likely to be a reflection of how wounded their parent or parents are, as they will be egocentric at this stage.

Another part of this is that personalising what took place and idealising one or both of their parents', will allow them to experience a false sense of control. This will show that, at this stage, they have the level of cognitive development required to be able to deceive themselves into believing that they can do something about what is going on and are not totally helpless, which will also serve as a defence to keep their pain and reality at bay.

The messages they hear directly through what their parent or parents' say and indirectly by how they behave will go straight into their mind. And, as they will believe that there is something inherently wrong with them and they are powerless and totally dependent, the only option they will have is to adapt to their environment and develop a disconnected false self that will allow them to survive.

This is not to say that how they respond won't be influenced by their temperament and how sensitive they are, for instance. But, as they are powerless and totally dependent, they are still going to have to adapt.

So, whether they do something or not is then largely going to depend on how their parent or parents' respond, as opposed to if it is in alignment with who they are. What is going on within them will end up being a mystery, and they will be focused on what is taking place externally.

This will cause them to experience a lot of pain, but, as time passes, they will soon lose touch with it and what happened, thanks to their brain's ability to repress pain and the memories that go with it. A way of behaving that they resisted at one point in time can then be what they accept as the years go by.

Nonetheless, no matter how many years have passed since that time in someone's life, their true self is still going to be within them. It can be covered up, but it won't disappear.

Moreover, the developmental needs that were not met all those years ago won't have simply disappeared either. Nevertheless, due to how alienated they can be from themselves, they might not be aware of them.

This will relate to their need to be cherished, cared for, wanted, loved, protected, touched, held, and seen, for example. From behind the scenes, so to speak, these needs will be driving their behaviour.

One way that these unmet developmental needs can influence their life is by them endlessly ending up in situations where they are deprived of what they need. This is because parts of them will cause them to unconsciously recreate situations that are very similar to their early experiences, so that they continue to struggle for love, in the hope that this time it will be different and they will finally receive what they missed out on.

But, as these situations will be very similar, not to mention the time for them to fulfil these unmet developmental needs will be over, this won't happen. How they felt all those years ago will end up being re-experienced.

They will then unconsciously struggle to meet their unmet developmental needs to avoid feeling how they felt when these needs were not met, only to re-experience how they felt all those years ago. As bizarre as this behaviour can appear to be, re-experiencing these feelings in this way - as opposed to feeling them in their original context and facing up to the fact that they will never receive the love that they missed out on (and letting go of their false hope in the process) - will be less painful.

Behaving in this way is then not going to make sense on one level but it will on another level. It is simply a way for their brain to protect them.

The downside is that it will cause them to suffer ad infinitum. It can be seen as the difference between a house that has a number of walls that continually fall down and a house that ends up falling down once and is then able to be built on solid foundations.

As they are not aware of what is going on, it is also not going to occur to them that although they were unable to face how they felt all those years ago, they are no longer the same person. Now that they are an adult, they can reach out for support to help them face how they feel; they are no longer alone.

Doing this would enable them to gradually develop their inner strength. And, before long, they would probably be able to face how they feel by themselves.

To get back to the main point, another way of looking at this process would be to say that they will be engaging in repetition compulsion. Their past will be over, but they will continue to be imprisoned by it, with them living in an emotional desert.

Yet, as they won't be consciously choosing to experience life in this way and their conscious mind will have forgotten about how they felt all those years ago, it is likely to be as though they are just unlucky and they can believe what is going on 'out there' has caused them to feel a certain way. They can feel totally hopeless and helpless, and this is how they felt all those years ago, as there was absolutely nothing that they could do.

What this also demonstrates is that while their conscious mind will see life in one way, their unconscious mind will see life in another way. To their conscious mind, it will be clear that another person is not their parent, but to their unconscious mind, it won't be clear.

This part of them won't have a sense of time and won't be able to see clearly, which is why the past can be effortlessly projected into the present. It wouldn't matter if a million years passed for this part of them, as it would still see life in the same way.

If this struggle for love wasn't taken into account and the focus was purely on their behaviour, and they are not seen as being unlucky, it would probably seem as though they are just sabotaging their life, and that this is due to them not having a sense of deserving. This will be part of it, but what will have the biggest impact is that if they were to have what they wanted, they would no longer be able to struggle.

This would cause them to come face to face with the fact that they won't receive what they missed out on and to feel helpless (this is why going through periods of being depressed is part of the healing journey and is not a sign that something is 'wrong'). Unlike the helplessness they would experience by meeting someone who can't love them, meeting someone who can is likely to unlock some of the deeper pain they felt during their formative years, but were unable to handle, and ended up being repressed.

Also, if they were to face up to the fact that they won't receive what they missed out on and face their wounds, they are likely to lose a lot of motivation. The fuel that was being created to allow them to avoid how they felt and to try to attain what couldn't be attained would start to subside, with them needing to find other sources of fuel to motivate them.

Lastly, if they were deeply traumatised right from the beginning of their life, so from the moment they were born, or whilst they were in their mother's womb, their true self might have withdrawn and practically died. What took place during this period of their development might then have been compounded by what took place when they were an infant, toddler, and/or child.

In this instance, it will take time for their true self to feel safe enough to come out of hiding, find the will to live, and slowly be reintegrated. This is why someone can have a fairly nurturing childhood and end up in a position where it appears as though this wasn't the case.

So, if you can see that you are out of touch with your true self or have a very weak connection to it, your life doesn't have to stay this way forever. This is something that part of you knows, or you wouldn't have invested in this book.

In 'the first part' section, I will look into some of the symptoms that are a reflection of the false self, and, in 'the second part' section, I will go into what you can do to gradually develop a strong connection with your true self and for it to be normal for you to reveal who you are.

The First Part

Examples Of The False Self

Chapter 1

Assertiveness

Do You Find It Hard To Assert Yourself?

As far as some people are concerned, the purpose of life is to be happy; whereas for others, it is to live a meaningful life. When it comes to the former, it is going to be all about feeling good.

Pleasure or Pain

So, when someone has this outlook, they may believe that the alternative is to feel bad. As a result of this, it is going to be normal for them to do everything they can to feel good.

What is then generally going to define whether or not they do something is how it will make them feel. One way of looking at this would be to say that this is going to be a very shallow existence.

A Deeper Experience

When it comes to the latter, someone may believe that the alternative would be for them to live a life that is meaningless. Consequently, it is going to be the norm for them to do what they can to make sure this doesn't happen.

And what will generally define whether or not they do something will depend on whether it is in alignment with their purpose. By being this way, they are likely to live a life of great depth.

A Closer Look

For this to take place, they will need to listen to their needs and do what they can to fulfil them. This will relate to their so-called lower needs and to their so-called higher needs.

What this means is that they will need to take care of themselves, and they will need to do what they can to fulfil their need to make a difference in the world. And, as surprising as this may sound, the only way that they will be able to truly make a difference in the world is if they look after themselves.

Balance

Making sure that they eat correctly, exercise, take the time to rest and have fulfilling personal relationships, for instance, will give them the energy to extend themselves to others. If they don't look after themselves, they are going to end up running on empty; said another way, they will be there for others, but they won't be there for themselves.

Being able to be there for others is one thing, but it is another thing altogether to do this without neglecting oneself. In order for them to be able to be there for themselves, they will need to value themselves and be comfortable with their own needs.

Another Component

It doesn't end there, though, as they will need to feel as though it is safe enough for them to fulfil their needs and to express themselves. There are likely to be moments when it would be easier for them to say yes than it would be for them to say no, and for them to simply go along with what others are doing.

This is when they will need to stand their ground and do something that won't necessarily please others. But even though there will be moments when something like this happens, it is not going to cause them to change their behaviour.

Part of Life

They could be aware of the fact that they are an individual, which is why it is not possible for them to always go along with what other people want them to do. If they were simply an extension of others, it would be different.

When someone experiences life in this way, they could believe that this is how everyone experiences life. However, if they were able to put their reality to one side, they might soon find out that this is not the case.

A Different Reality

Here, someone is going to behave as though they don't have their own needs and feelings, and this is going to make it difficult for them to live a fulfilling life. Whether they say yes or no is typically going to depend on what is taking place externally.

Doing what they can to please others is going to be their priority, meaning that their needs will be of secondary importance. And, while this will allow them to please others from time to time, what it won't do is allow them to please themselves.

Conflict

Part of them is going to have the need to do what they can to please others, and another part of them is going to want to fulfil their own needs. Ultimately, having the desire to solely please others is not natural.

The reason for this is that they are not working with themselves; they are working against themselves. Still, this is not something that has just happened; it is likely to show that there was a time in their life when it wasn't safe for them to listen to their own needs and to go about fulfilling them.

Way Back

If they were to take a step back and think about what took place when they were growing up, they may find that this was a time when it wasn't safe for them to assert themselves. Therefore, they would have had to hide their true self.

Chapter 2

Being Seen

Do You Hide?

It could be said that whenever someone spends time around others, they are going to be seen. Therefore, the only way for them not to be seen by others will be to spend time by themselves.

Black and White

This is then something that is not hard to understand; in fact, it is perfectly clear. With this in mind, if someone doesn't want to be seen by others, it is going to mean that they will have to isolate themselves from the world.

On the other hand, if someone does want to be seen by others, they will simply need to make sure that they spend time around people. To understand this, there is going to be no need for someone to use a lot of brain power.

Hidden In Plain Sight

Nevertheless, although this might seem to be the case, there is far more to this than meets the eye. What this comes down to is that someone doesn't need to isolate themselves in order to hide.

The only thing that they need to do is to spend time around others, but to make sure that other people don't see them. When this takes place, they are not going to want to draw attention to themselves.

19

Three Parts

There can be the kind of clothes they wear, their body language, and what their energy is like. Each one of these elements will have a part to play, and they might not even have to think about any of them.

They could have been this way for so long that it is no longer necessary for them to consciously think about what they need to do to hide. When it comes to their clothes, they may typically wear dark colours.

Invisible

Wearing grey or black, for instance, can allow them to fade into the background. They could often have closed body language, giving off the message that they don't want to be approached, and they may also find it hard to maintain eye contact.

Energetically, it could be as though they are somewhere else, and this is because they may find it hard to embrace the present moment. Most of their attention could be in their mind, or it might even seem as though it is somewhere else entirely.

A Number of Things

It is then not just one thing that will allow this person to merge into the background; it is a combination of things. What this illustrates is that being noticed is not just about being around others.

And even though someone like this has the need to hide, it doesn't mean that every part of them is on board with this. Another part of them will probably have the need to be seen, but this is likely to be overshadowed by their need to hide.

Inner Conflict

This part of them is going to be in control, and this is going to cause them to experience a certain amount of pain. The part of them that wants to be seen will be their true self.

This is the part of them that relates to their true needs and feelings, whereas their false self relates to a role that they play to survive. Playing this role can allow them to 'fit in', yet what it won't do is allow them to live a life that is worth living.

Another Area

Consequently, their relationships are unlikely to be very fulfilling – how could they be if they don't feel comfortable enough to be seen? They are likely to play a role when they are around their friends, thereby ignoring their true needs and feelings.

They could be drawn to people who are comfortable with attention, making it easy for them to stay in the shadows. These people might treat them reasonably well, or they could have the tendency to mistreat them.

A Closer Look

Although behaving in this way is having a negative effect on their life, it is going to be what feels safe. So, if they were to change their behaviour, they could end up experiencing fear, anxiety, and shame, amongst other things.

It can be hard to understand why someone would experience so much fear, especially when having the need to be seen is part of being human. What this is likely to show is that there was a time in their life when it wasn't safe for them to express themselves.

More Than Once

At the same time, they may have had a number of moments in their life when it wasn't safe enough for them to assert themselves. If this relates to what happened when they were younger, this may have been what it was like day after day, year after year.

This may have been a time when they were abused and/or neglected, and this would have caused them to be deeply traumatised. Being seen would have been associated with something that would put their life at risk.

Chapter 3

Boundaries

Do You Lack Boundaries?

What is clear is that when someone has boundaries, their life is going to be a lot better than it would be if they didn't have them. The reason for this is that they have their own needs and feelings.

So, while they are going to be an interdependent human being who needs other people, that doesn't mean that they will always want to do what other people are doing. This is going to apply to the people they are close to, as well as to the people they don't know very well.

Drawing the Line

Naturally, there are going to be moments when they are interested in doing what one of their friends or family members wants them to do. For example, one could be asked if they would like to go out for the day, and this could be something that they are only too happy to do.

At other times, they might have other things going on, or they just might not want to do something. Here, they will pay attention to what is taking place within them and let the other person know that they can't make it.

The Outcome

Behaving in this way might cause them to displease the other person, or it might not bother them. Yet, even if it does have a negative effect on them, it doesn't mean that they have done something wrong.

Ultimately, they will have listened to their own needs, and this is in their best interest. It is not their responsibility to please other people; if it were, there would be no reason for them to have boundaries.

An Empty Shell

In this case, they would be nothing more than an extension of other people, and so their purpose on this earth would be to fulfil other people's needs. Saying yes, not no, would be the only thing they would need to say.

However, as they do have their own needs and feelings, it proves that they are not on this planet to please other people. Now, this is not to say that they will only think about their own needs and ignore other people's needs.

Give And Take

Life is, after all, about being there for ourselves and being there for others; if someone only focused on their own needs, they would have a pretty empty and lonely existence. Still, it can be easy for someone to believe that one only thinks about themselves when they pay attention to their own needs.

What this could show is that they have the tendency to focus on other people's needs, or that fulfilling their needs is just a normal part of their life. And through taking care of their own needs, they might not even be aware of what it would be like to neglect them.

Protection

Therefore, when someone has the ability to say no, it is going to stop them from being walked over. And as they are inherently vulnerable, it is going to be vital for them to look after themselves.

If someone didn't have this ability, it wouldn't matter if another person wanted to walk over them or not. What this comes down to is that if someone doesn't let another person know that they don't want to do something, there will be no need for this person to change their behaviour.

A Clear Message

By speaking up and standing their ground, they will be letting someone know when they don't want to do something. And if this is someone who has no interest in walking over others, they will be pleased that one has made this clear.

But while having boundaries is the ideal, it doesn't mean that everyone on this planet has them. When someone doesn't have them, there is a strong chance that they have always experienced life in this way.

The Norm

One could believe that they don't have a say when it comes to how other people treat them, and that they have to please them. Their needs are then going to be put to one side, and their priority will be to fulfil other people's needs.

From the outside, it could then seem as though they are a selfless human being and that they are doing the right thing, but this is going to be nothing more than an illusion. If a closer look were taken, it would be clear that they are neglecting themselves.

Two Parts

They are then not simply a selfless human being; they are someone who is too concerned with other people's needs and feelings. In addition to this, they could have people in their life who are abusive.

This is likely to mean that they are used to feeling angry, frustrated and as though they have no control over their life. Thus, it is going to be a challenge for them to feel good about themselves and their life.

The Main Difference

If they were to get in touch with what is taking place within them, they are likely to find that behaving in this way is what feels safe. It might be hard for them to understand why this is, especially as this is causing them to suffer.

Then again, they might be only too aware of why this is what feels safe. What they may find is that their early years were a time when they were walked over by their parent or parents'.

In The Beginning

During this time, their parent or parents' wouldn't have been able to accept the fact that they had their own needs and feelings. It wouldn't have mattered if they wanted to do something, as they wouldn't have had a choice.

They would then have learnt that it wasn't safe for them to listen to their own needs and feelings – if they did, it would have caused them to experience even more pain. Consequently, they would have had to develop a false self.

Chapter 4

Confidence

Do You Only Feel Confident When You Play A Role?

In order for someone to be themselves, it will be necessary for them to feel confident enough to do so. Therefore, if this is not in place, it is not going to be possible for them to express their true self.

One way of looking at it would be to say that their true self is the top of a table, and the confidence they have to express this part of them is the legs that support it. So, in the same way that they wouldn't be able to be themselves if they didn't feel confident, the table wouldn't be able to be used without its legs.

A Waste of Time

As a result of this, it is easy to see why telling someone to just 'be themselves' is not always going to work. If someone were to hear this and they didn't feel confident, it could end up bouncing straight off them.

They are then not going to be able to follow this advice unless they start to feel different about themselves. Yet, if the other person doesn't realise this, they could wonder what the problem is.

A Lack of Empathy

This could be someone who has been able to be themselves for as long as they can remember. And as this is what is normal for them, they are unable to put themselves in another person's shoes, so to speak.

By being this way, one is unlikely to feel as though this is someone who understands what they are going through. If anything, they could feel as though this person is trying to undermine them.

Hidden

One is going to be someone who comes across as having no confidence, and their true self will be covered up. They are then going to be used to doing what other people want, and this means that their needs are generally going to be overlooked.

Other people could typically describe them as being shy or reserved, and they might even see them as being introverted. There is then a strong chance that they will be a follower, as opposed to a leader.

An Empty Existence

Through doing what other people want and not having the ability to do what they want, their life is unlikely to be very fulfilling. They could be used to feeling frustrated, powerless, and helpless.

They could feel as though they were on the sidelines, watching other people live the kind of life that they wanted to live. And while they could have people around them who understand what is taking place, they could also be surrounded by people who don't.

Trapped

What this will then do is stop them from getting the support that they need, and they could feel as though these people hold them back. This is because they won't be able to see them for who they are.

There is a chance these people are also out of touch with themselves, and this is why they are not aware of what is taking place. Nevertheless, if one doesn't reveal their true self, it is to be expected that they will be treated in this way.

Another Dynamic

However, if they don't feel comfortable enough to reveal their true self, it doesn't mean that they will come across in this way. Instead, they can end up coming across as someone who has it all together.

Yet, as they don't feel comfortable enough to be themselves, it can be hard to believe how they can come across this way. Due to how they feel, there is going to be no reason for them to be this way.

A Role

What this is likely to come down to is that they will be putting on an act, and this act will allow them to receive approval from others. Receiving this approval will allow them to come across as confident.

At a deeper level, they are going to be the same as the person above, but that's the only thing they will have in common. Having a false self that allows them to be accepted by others stops them from having to face how they feel.

Two Sides

So, on one side, this will allow them to fit in, but on the other, it is still going to stop them from being able to listen to themselves. From the outside, it can seem as though they live life on their own terms, but this will be nothing more than an illusion.

Ergo, if other people no longer responded to them in the same way, they would soon end up falling down. It will be as if they were being pumped up by other people's responses, and now these responses are no longer there, they will have deflated.

A Different Experience

If, on the other hand, they were in touch with their true self and they felt comfortable expressing this part of themselves, this wouldn't take place. How they come across to others wouldn't be an act.

It would be built on firm foundations, and they wouldn't need other people to approve of them. The strength they have to be themselves would come from within, and there would be no reason for them to hide.

A Closer Look

What can define whether someone feels comfortable enough to be themselves, or not, can be what took place during their early years.

Chapter 5

People Pleasing

Do You Try To Please Others?

When someone has the ability to go along to get along, it can be a lot easier for them to get on with others. By not having the desire to rock the boat, so to speak, they are rarely going to rub other people up the wrong way.

This is likely to mean that they will have a number of friends and that it won't be difficult for them to make even more as time goes by. If another person were asked what they like about them, they could point to the fact that they are easy to be around.

Zero Conflict

Their time together is typically going to be harmonious, and this will allow the other person to take control, that's if they want to. They won't need to worry about whether or not one will resist.

One will be seen as someone who is likely to go along with just about whatever they decide to do, which is why it will allow the other person to fulfil their own needs. So, while they might have more friends than someone who doesn't behave in this manner, it is not going to be a bed of roses.

A loss of self

By behaving in this manner, it is going to be a challenge for them to express their true self. Their primary need will be to get on with others, which is going to cause them to neglect their other needs.

If they don't want to experience conflict, the last thing they are going to want to do is to assert themselves. What this would do is cause other people to respond to them in a different manner.

A New Experience

As a result of being agreeable, they will be used to receiving positive responses from other people. This will have a positive effect on their wellbeing, giving them the encouragement that they need to behave in the same way.

But if they were to no longer act in this manner, the amount of positive feedback that they receive from others is likely to decrease. And, if they find it hard to feel good about themselves unless they please others, this is going to be hard for them to handle.

Another Outcome

At the same time, the very idea of displeasing others could be enough to stop them in their tracks. Therefore, while pleasing others will cause them to overlook their own needs, it will be seen as the only option.

It is then going to be as if the part of them that wants to live in an authentic manner is not strong enough. Until this is no longer the case, they will continue to focus on other people's needs.

Part of Life

If they were simply an extension of others, there would be no reason for them to change their behaviour. The main purpose of their existence would be to tune into other people's needs and to do what they could to fulfil them.

But as they are not on this planet to do this, it is going to mean that there will be moments when they won't please others. That is, of course, if they pay attention to their own needs.

True Fulfilment

When they pay attention to their own needs and do what they can to fulfil them, their life is going to be far more fulfilling than it would be otherwise. Now, this is not to say that they will no longer care about others, far from it.

What this comes down to is that they won't be completely focused on other people; they will be more in balance. There will be moments when others don't approve of how they behave, but then there will be moments when they don't approve of how other people behave.

Out of Balance

If someone only cared about their own needs and found it hard to be there for others, it would be necessary for them to move from one side of the spectrum to the middle. Yet, when one behaves in the opposite manner, they will need to move from the other side of the spectrum to the middle.

One is then not going from one extreme to the other when they are in touch with their true self; they are simply embracing the part of their nature that has been overlooked for so long. The part of their nature that is likely to be undeveloped is their masculine aspect.

A Different Energy

This is the part of them that will give them the strength to assert themselves in the world. One of the main reasons why they would find it difficult to do this is that they don't feel safe in their body.

Their need to please others is then a sign that they don't feel safe enough to stand their ground. If this is the case, it can show that there was a time in their life when it was far too dangerous for them to express themselves.

It has served its Purpose

Perhaps they were brought up in an environment where they were abused and/or neglected, for instance. It would then have been essential for them to behave as though they were just an extension of others.

Behaving in this way would have been a matter of life or death, and not something that they had a lot of control over. Nevertheless, while it kept them alive at this time in their life, it is no longer necessary for them to behave in this way.

Chapter 6

Relationships

Do You Act Like You Have It All Together?

On the one hand, there is going to be how someone behaves, and on the other, there is going to be how someone feels on the inside. At times, what is taking place within them will be expressed through how they behave.

An Authentic Human Being

In this case, they are generally not going to put on an act around others. Ultimately, they are going to be in touch with their true self, with this being primarily made up of their needs, feelings, and preferences.

So, when they are around others, there will be no need for them to spend a lot of time thinking about what is, or what isn't, an acceptable way to behave. They can pay attention to what is going on within them, along with being aware of what is going on around them, and they can then decide how they will behave.

The Present Moment

Being in touch with their inner world and having the ability to express who they are is going to allow them to save a lot of energy. Along with this, it will also stop them from having to experience too much pressure.

The reason for this is that they won't have to spend an endless amount of time going over how they will behave around people, which is likely to reduce the amount of stress that they experience. They are then bound to come into contact with people who can sense how authentic they are.

A Match

When another person does appreciate them for being this way, it could show that they are also in touch with their true self and feel comfortable enough to reveal who they are to others. Then again, it might be a sign that this person wants to experience life in this way.

As a result of this, this person might be aware of who they are, but they could find it hard to reveal who they are when they are around others. And, if one is an authentic human being, they are going to be drawn to people who are the same.

Intimacy

The ability that they have to connect to each part of their own being will be what allows them to deeply connect to other people. Talking about what they have done each day or what they want to achieve, for instance, is not going to be as far as it will go.

They will have the need to go much deeper, and this will include talking about how they feel about certain things, looking deeply into life, and questioning their own motives, amongst other things. One might have been this way for as long as they can remember, or they might not have been this way for very long.

A Different Experience

At other times, what is taking place within someone won't be expressed through how they behave. How they come across is then going to be radically different from what is taking place within them.

What this is likely to mean is that they are generally out of touch with a number of their needs and feelings. This is then why they are able to behave in a way that goes against what is truly going on for them.

A Strong Shell

When something like this takes place, someone can come across as strong and create the impression that they have it all together. This may mean that they also have a muscular physique, with this being another way for them to create this impression in others.

Due to how they come across, there could be a number of people who describe them as being "charismatic". These people could see them as some kind of role model and aspire to be like them.

Another Area

If this is the case, it could also mean that they have a very successful career. One is then not going to be short of money, and they may have the kind of possessions that are often said to be what someone has if they have 'made it'.

Nevertheless, while this person can appear to be incredibly strong, there is likely to be one area that will give them away, so to speak.

If someone were to take a closer look at what their relationships are like, they may soon realise that something isn't right.

A Shallow Experience

But as they are generally going to be out of touch with themselves, this is to be expected. One is then likely to have relationships with others that are surface-level, and if they do end up in an intimate relationship, the other person could be needy and emotionally unstable.

The Mirror

Other people could then question how someone so strong could end up with someone who comes across as being so weak. Then again, this could be put down to the fact that opposites attract.

Yet, if these people were aware of what was taking place within this person at a deeper level, they might realise that this person's partner is expressing that which one has repressed. The neediness and emotional instability one person shows are simply a reflection of what the other person has disconnected from.

Self-Protection

Taking this into account, the reason one has created such a hard shell around them is that they feel so vulnerable on the inside. And there is a strong chance that this shell, or armouring, was created at a very young age, an age where this was the only thing that they could do to protect themselves.

Chapter 7

Relationships

Do You Neglect Your Own Needs When You Are In A Relationship?

Although someone could pay attention to a number of their own needs when they are single, this could be something that changes when they are in a relationship. It could then be said that they will be there for themselves when they are single and end up abandoning themselves when they are not.

Two Problems

Therefore, when they are single, they might think about what it would be like to be in a relationship. Yet, when they are in a relationship, they could spend a lot of energy thinking about what it would be like to be single again.

Due to what they go through in each experience, it could be a challenge for them to feel at peace. At the same time, when they are in a relationship, they might not be aware of how they feel.

The Priority

The reason for this is that they could be so caught up in doing what they can to meet the other person's needs that they completely ignore what is taking place within them. And even if they do have moments when they do tune into how they feel, this could be something that rarely takes place.

They are then going to be behaving as though they are nothing more than an extension of the other person. Their purpose will be to do just about everything they can to meet the other person's needs.

A Role

It is then not going to matter what they did to meet their own needs before they were in a relationship, as they will now have something else to do that is more important. This could be something that their partner is completely on board with, or they might wonder what is going on.

If their partner does have a problem with it, it still doesn't mean that they will be able to change their behaviour. Instead, they could make out that it is fine and continue to behave in the same way.

Self-Centred

Alternatively, their partner could believe that other people exist to take care of their own needs, which is going to stop them from changing their behaviour. If this is the case, there is going to be no reason for them to try to get one to change.

If anything, they are going to reward this behaviour, and this is going to show that they believe that their needs are the only needs that are important. It might not even occur to them that other people have needs.

Down Hill

It is perfectly clear that when someone is in a relationship like this, it is not going to add anything to their life; the only thing that it is going to do is wear them down. There is going to be an effect this has on their wellbeing and their life in general.

Before they were in the relationship, their life could have been going in the right direction. But as the weeks and months go by, their life will end up getting progressively worse.

The Next Step

If they were able to get to the point where they can no longer tolerate what is taking place, they might be able to end the relationship. This could be a time when they will begin to get back in touch with their own needs, and as a result of this, their life could start to improve.

After a short time, they could end up getting into another relationship, and the same thing could take place all over again. This could then be the second time that this has taken place, or it could be something that has happened on other occasions.

A Victim

One way of looking at this would be to say that this person just happens to end up with people who are self-centred. Consequently, there is only going to be so much that they can do; they will need to wait until the right person appears in their life.

If this is the outlook that they have, it is not going to be much of a surprise for them to feel powerless, helpless, and as though they have no control over this area of their life. What this wouldn't take into consideration, though, is that they are not simply an observer of their reality (even though this is the impression that their mind and eyes will create).

The Common Denominator

At the end of the day, there is one person who keeps showing up, and that is the person they see whenever they look in the mirror. With this in mind, it is going to be essential for them to look into why they neglect their own needs when they get into a relationship.

They might also see that they find it hard to fulfil their own needs even when they are not in a relationship. Either way, what this could show is that they don't feel safe enough to pay attention to their own needs or believe that they deserve to have them met.

A Deeper Look

Focusing on someone else's needs and doing what they can to fulfil them is going to be what feels safe. It can then be hard for them to comprehend why they wouldn't feel safe enough to pay attention to their own needs or be deserving of having them met

However, if they were to think about what their early years were like, they may begin to understand why they behave in this way. This may have been a time in their life when they had to focus on their parent or parents' needs, with them being placed in a parental role.

Chapter 8

Relationships

Do You Play A Role?

Although there are going to be moments in someone's life when they will need to be serious, they won't need to behave in this way all the time. Along with this, they will need to be easy-going at times, and at other times, they will need to be firm.

Multifaceted

Ultimately, how someone will need to behave can all depend on what kind of environment they are in and what the context is. Yet, as they are going to have more than one side to their nature, it is not going to be a challenge for them to adapt and to change their behaviour.

Through being this way, it is going to be a lot easier for them to handle the different challenges that life has to offer and as well as to enjoy the good experiences that come their way. This is not to say that they can't enjoy a challenge; what it comes down to is that there are going to be moments that are not challenging.

Playtime

For example, if they were to go for a night out or to have a drink with a few friends, it is unlikely to be a challenge. During this time, it will be important for them to be able to relax and be in the moment.

It probably won't be necessary for them to behave as they would at work; if they did, they might not be able to embrace the time that they spend together. This is then no different from how they are not always going to wear the same clothes.

Flexibility

The kind of clothes that they wear will also depend on what they are going to do and who they are going to see. This is not simply a case of 'fitting in'; if it were, then wearing the same clothes all the time would be a sign of strength and defiance.

At times, the clothes they wear will stop them from injuring themselves, and at other times, they will allow them to create the right impression. Therefore, if they wore the same clothes all the time, they would be doing more harm than good.

The Right Tool

So, whether it relates to how they behave or the kind of clothes they wear, it will be no different from using the right tool for a job. This will be the same as how someone would use a saw to cut a piece of wood or a hammer to bang a nail in.

On the one hand, they will realise what kind of tool they need to use, and on the other, the tool that they need will be available. And when it comes to their ability to change their behaviour, it will show that they know how they need to behave and that they have the ability to change their behaviour.

A Choice

Still, this doesn't mean that they will just be a chameleon, as this would mean that their behaviour is being completely defined by their environment. If this is what happened, it would show that they have a weak sense of self.

The difference is that they are choosing to change their behaviour, and this means that there may be moments when they don't want to adapt. Perhaps they are not in the mood, and this will then cause them to come across differently.

The Reason

What this will show is that they feel safe enough to change their behaviour, and this is why they don't always need to go along with how other people behave. If this weren't the case, it would be normal for them to be a chameleon.

They will feel as though it is safe for them to exist, and this will play a big part in what will allow them to embrace their true self. Now, this doesn't mean that they will be aware of this, as they may have felt this way their whole life.

The Norm

When someone can behave how they want to behave, it is going to make it a lot easier for them to live a fulfilling existence. They will be aware of what their needs are, and they will have the ability to fulfil them.

There are then going to be people who have the tendency to behave as other people want them to (and how they think they want them to). This can mean that they will always behave in the same way.

A Role

They may generally come across as someone who is only too happy to please others, and this is likely to mean they will be easy-going. Or, they could always feel down and not show a lot of emotion.

In addition to how they behave, there can also be how well they do in life. They may find that they only feel comfortable staying at a certain level and, if they go any higher, it causes them to experience fear and anxiety.

Trapped

They are then going to be a multifaceted human being, but they will act as though they only have one or a few sides to their nature. This is then going to be no different from a builder who only has a few tools; they are not going to be able to do the job properly.

It can then seem as though they are living their life, yet this is not going to be the complete truth. They won't be able to embrace their needs, and this is going to stop them from being able to live a fulfilling life.

A Closer Look

At a deeper level, this is going to be what feels safe, and unless this changes, they will continue to play a role. What this can show is that they had to play a role in order to survive when they were younger.

If they changed their behaviour, it may have caused them to be abused and/or neglected by their parent or parents'. There may have been moments when playing this role didn't keep them safe either.

Chapter 9

Relationships

Do You Try To Fix Others?

It is often said that the best thing that someone can do for another person when they are going through a challenging time is to simply be there for them. So, when they are in the other person's presence, it will be vital for them to be completely present.

No Agenda

This means that they are not doing anything; they are simply being in the moment. They can then let go and not have to worry about whether or not this person's life will change or get better.

What this can also show is that they believe that this person is capable of sorting out their own life and that it is not their responsibility to 'fix' them. By being this way, it is likely to show that they have good boundaries.

A Clear Line

They will know where they begin and end, and where other people begin and end. As a result of this, it is going to stop them from trying to define how other people live their lives.

In this context, they will realise that it is not down to them to tell the other person what they should do. This will also allow them to treat the other person as an adult, as opposed to a powerless child.

51

A Reflection

And, as they don't treat other people as though they are missing something, it is likely to show that they feel comfortable in their own skin. They will probably understand, at a deeper level, that their value is not based on what they do.

Therefore, the reason why they don't see the other person as being incapable is due to the fact that they don't see themselves in this way. Still, this doesn't mean that they won't do anything for them if they are asked.

A Huge Difference

When this happens, they are not giving unsolicited advice; they are being asked to give their advice. They are then going to be coming from a different place, which means that their advice will be presented differently.

The other person is likely to feel acknowledged and as though they are valued and respected. And if they are going through a tough time, there is a strong chance that this is exactly how they want to feel in their presence.

A Rare Occurrence

It could be said that the above scenario is the ideal; even so, this is not something that always takes place. In a lot of cases, there is a far greater chance that someone will tell another person what to do.

Someone can find out that another person is going through a tough time, and it can be as though they are some kind of superhero. It is not going to be possible for them to lend an ear, so to speak, as they will have to use their mouth.

One Intention

Their ears won't have a purpose at this point, and their main aim will be to do what they can to fix this person. This whole process will be about doing, not being, which means that they are not going to take the time to tune into what the other person is going through.

In a way, they won't see the other person as an individual; they will see them as an extension of themselves. They might not even know where they begin and end, and where other people begin and end.

Two Factors

When someone has the need to 'fix' others, it can be due to at least two reasons. Firstly, this can be a sign that they believe that their value is defined by what they do and not by who they are.

Consequently, if they don't solve someone else's problems, they are likely to feel bad about themselves. Secondly, seeing another person in pain can unconsciously remind them of their own pain that they have lost touch with.

Caught Up

If they were to take a step back and no longer try to solve other people's problems, they might end up being overwhelmed by their own pain. It is then as if they are trying to clean their window by cleaning their neighbour's window.

This is, of course, a complete waste of time. Clearly, the only way that they will be able to solve their own problems is by fixing them directly, not by trying to solve other people's problems.

Two Benefits

Focusing on their own issues will be more painful in the short-term, but it will make their life a lot better in the long-term. Not only this, but the people they come into contact with are more likely to appreciate their company.

Instead of feeling as though their boundaries are not being respected and that they are not being heard, for instance, they will be able to feel respected, valued, and heard. The only thing that they will have done for this to take place is to be completely present; nothing more, nothing less.

The Challenge

If they believe that their value is based on what they do, there is a chance that their upbringing set them up to believe this. This may have been a time when they had to fulfil their parent or parents' needs.

Being there for others would have been a matter of survival. Their true self wouldn't have been able to see the light of day, causing them to automatically create a false self.

Chapter 10

Relationships

Do You Try To Rescue Others?

While some people take the time to be there for themselves and to be there for others, there are others who don't. If someone can relate to the former, they are not going to have the tendency to neglect themselves; whereas if they can relate to the latter, this will be the norm.

Two Options

The trouble is that when someone is focused on other people's needs, they can believe that they only have two options. Either they focus on themselves or they focus on others, and focusing on themselves is going to be seen as being selfish.

Focusing on others, on the other hand, is likely to be seen as being selfless. So, as they believe that they only have two choices, it is not surprising that they behave in this manner.

An Unconscious Choice

At the same time, this doesn't mean that this is something that they will think about all the time. In fact, they might not even reflect on how they are behaving; this will then be something that just happens.

Being there for others is going to be who they are, and there is a strong chance that this kind of behaviour will allow them to receive a lot of positive feedback. Receiving this feedback can make it easier for them to keep their true feelings at bay.

Now and Then

At the end of the day, no matter how much positive feedback they receive, it is not going to change the fact that they are ignoring themselves. Due to this, there can be moments when they will feel frustrated and angry, and they might even feel depressed from time to time.

The 'negative' emotions that they experience through not fulfilling their own needs will have been pushed out of their conscious awareness, with this being the reason why they will feel down or flat, for instance. But, unless they take a deeper look and change their behaviour, they are not going to be able to do anything about this.

Business as Usual

Yet while this would be the ideal, they are more likely to carry on as normal. They will soon find someone else (or the same person) who needs to be saved or rescued, thereby allowing them to run away from how they feel.

What is also going to make it harder for them to change is that this kind of behaviour is so common in today's world. A lot of relationships, for instance, are made up of someone who acts like they need to be saved and someone who acts like it is their job to save them.

Part of Life

It can then seem as though some people on this planet are empowered, while others are not. This would be an accurate assessment, yet the people who are truly empowered are not going to be rescuing others.

What this comes down to is that people are empowered through being given the guidance and support that they need to stand on their own two feet, not through having someone else do everything for them. The only thing that this will do is stop them from being able to go from a dependent to an interdependent human being.

A Dysfunctional Dynamic

Therefore, whether one is in a relationship with someone who acts like they need to be rescued and/or they are trying to rescue their friends, for instance, they are likely to be doing more harm than good. Taking this into account, it can be hard to understand why they would continue to behave in this way if they are stopping these people from being able to take control of their own lives.

If they were to take a step back and look into why they behave in this manner, they may find that this is a way for them to indirectly fulfil their own needs. One is then going to feel ashamed of their needs and guilty if they try to express them, with this being the reason why they can't fulfil them directly.

The Defining Moment

Having needs is just part of being human; it is not something that anyone on this planet should be ashamed of or feel guilty about. Ergo, if someone does feel uncomfortable with their own needs, it is likely to show that there was a time in their life when they were not allowed to have needs.

Perhaps they were brought up by a parent who used them to fulfil their own needs, instead of giving them what they needed in order to grow and develop. One would then have had to take on the role of the parent and give up on being a child.

Out of Balance

Taking on this role would have meant that their purpose was to give and not to receive. Having this role may also have caused them to believe that they need to look strong, to be in control and that their value is based on what they do.

The role that they had to play during this time in their life to survive will be the role that they now play in their adult life. Their true self will have been covered up, and in its place will be a false self.

Letting Go

If they were to stop playing this role, they might end up getting in touch with a lot of pain, and this pain will come from the wounded parts that are within them. These parts will tell them everything they need to know about what happened to them throughout their formative years.

Chapter 11

Self-Care

Do You Find It Hard To Relax?

In today's world, it is not uncommon for someone to have a very busy life, and this can stop them from being able to just be. During the week, there is likely to be a certain amount of time that they are at work each day, and once they get home, they may have other things to do.

Another Job

This could be a time when they will have to do things for work, and this could show that this is something that takes over their whole life. But even if they don't have any work to do when they are at home, they could soon be taking part in some kind of exercise.

There is a chance that this will take up most of their evening, and they will need to find time to have something to eat. Once this takes place, it might not be long until it is time for them to go to bed.

No Different

They might then spend a lot of time counting down the days until the weekend, and they could think about what they will do. This part of their week is then going to be a time when they are able to take it easy and recharge their batteries, so to speak.

Having said that, this might not be what happens; instead, they might spend their weekends working. Or, if this doesn't happen, they could have so much going on that it stops them from being able to use this time to relax.

Stuck On a Treadmill

If they were to take a step back from it all, they could feel as though they were no longer a human being. They might see that it would be more accurate to describe themselves as a human doing.

So, although they are not a machine, they are going to be behaving like one. And what might also come to mind is that even machines need to rest; if they don't, they will end up burned out.

Self-Reflection

Upon realising this, they could look into what they can do to live their life differently. This would show that they have had enough of experiencing life in this way and that it is now time for them to live like a human being.

At the same time, they might be in a position where they are fed up with how their life is, but that could be as far as it will go. They will then get back on the treadmill, so to speak, and it might only be a matter of time before they step back again.

The Norm

If they just carry on with how their life is, they might not come across anyone who encourages them to change their life. What this comes down to is that they could be surrounded by people who experience life in the same way.

On the plus side, there is the chance that they will be able to complain about their life to these people. Now, this won't change anything, but what it will do is allow them to let off a bit of steam.

External Support

What they may find is that they are able to relax if they drink alcohol or take another substance. But unless they consume something like this, it is a challenge for them to just let go and embrace the moment.

If they were to do this, it could cause them to feel uncomfortable, and this might give them the urge to do something. It might then be accurate to say that it is not that they don't have time to relax; a big part of them doesn't want to relax.

By Design

Therefore, even though living in this way is causing them to experience a lot of stress, it is going to be what feels comfortable. Furthermore, if they feel this way when they relax, there is a chance that there is a reason why their job takes up most of their life.

It is then not that they just happen to have a job where they don't have a lot of time to just be; it is that they unconsciously chose a job like this. They can then feel as though they have no control over their life, but this will be nothing more than an illusion.

A Human Being

When someone can relax and enjoy doing nothing, they can find it hard to understand why this wouldn't be the case for everyone. This will show that they are able to just be, and they have the ability to take action.

One thing this is likely to illustrate is that one values themselves, and this will play a big part in why they don't need to always be doing something. On the other hand, when someone doesn't feel this way, it can be incredibly difficult for them to just be.

A Human Doing

This is likely to be a time when they will have to face how they feel about themselves, and this is likely to cause them to experience a lot of pain. But taking action will typically allow them to keep their feelings at bay.

If they were to just be with their feelings, they might end up feeling completely worthless, hopeless and helpless. Taking action is then not just going to be a way for them to avoid how they feel; it will also be a way for them to feel good and experience a sense of control.

External Self-Worth

Through being out of touch with their inherent value, it is then going to be normal for them to believe that their value is based on what they do. They could still be seen as someone who has it all together, but this is not going to be the truth.

The motivation that they have to achieve things is then going to be fuelled by their need to avoid how they feel at a deeper level; it will be coming from a place of emptiness, not wholeness. Thus, if they no longer felt worthless and felt whole, there would be no reason for them to behave in the same way.

The Cause

This can show that they didn't receive the kind of care that they needed to be able to develop in the right way very early on. This would have caused them to believe that there was something inherently wrong with them and to develop a false self in the process.

Chapter 12

Self-Expression

Do You Hide How You Feel?

If someone wanted to explain something to another person, there are a number of ways for them to do so. It could be said that the most important thing will be for them to use words, as this will allow them to be understood.

In addition to this, they can use their body and their emotions. Now, these two parts are clearly not essential, but what they will do is bring what they have to say to life.

A Big Difference

By utilising their body and emotions, it will be a lot easier for the other person to pay attention to what they have to say. It then might not matter if what they have to say is not very interesting.

What this comes down to is that what someone says is rarely as important as how they say it. So, if someone knows how to express themselves, there is a greater chance that other people will listen to them.

Part of Life

When someone feels comfortable with their emotions, it will be normal for them to behave in this manner. This can show that they have a healthy relationship with their emotions, and this is why they don't need to reject this part of their nature.

65

Consequently, there is a chance that they will also be happy to express how they feel. By being this way, they won't need to ignore how they feel and always come across as stoic.

A Time and A Place

This doesn't mean that they will always express how they feel, as there are going to be moments in their life when this is not going to be a good idea. For example, if they had a job where they had to serve customers, they would not always be able to express how they feel.

As if a customer were to cause problems, it would be necessary for them to act in a civilised manner. If they were to allow their emotions to get the better of them, it might end up causing even more problems.

A Choice

However, moments like these are going to be the exception as opposed to the rule, as they won't always behave in this way. They will have the freedom to express how they feel, and this is likely to have a positive effect on all of their relationships.

Not only will it be easier for other people to pay attention to what they have to say, but it will be easier for people to connect to them. After all, it is not just ideas that connect people; it is also how they feel.

A Deeper Connection

If they were to think about the people in their life who they have a strong connection, they are likely to find that they share how they feel with them and that these people do the same. It is through sharing how they feel that they will be able to have such a strong connection.

On the other hand, if they were to think about the people in their life with who they don't have this kind of connection, they may find that they only talk about surface-level things. They could talk about what they have been doing, plan to do, and what's taking place in the world, but that's about it.

Another Part

Still, this is not to say that they can form a strong connection with someone by just expressing how they feel, as it is not that black and white. Naturally, there are going to be other things that need to be in place.

For one thing, it will be a good idea for them to have the same values; having similar interests will also help. Thus, it will be a challenge for them to form a strong connection with someone if they don't express how they feel.

Comfortable

So, if they are going through a challenging time in their life, they could get in touch with a friend and express what's going on and how they feel. During this time, they are being vulnerable, and it could be said that this takes a lot of courage.

Another way of looking at it would be to say that what this shows is that they feel comfortable enough to open up. Regardless of what they are going through, they will be able to open up to the people they are close to.

Another Experience

It then doesn't take a lot of brain power to see that if someone can't express how they feel, their life is going to be very different. They are then going to be happy to share what is taking place at a more surface-level, but that will generally be as far as it will go.

From the outside, it might seem as though nothing ever affects them, and there could be people who see this as a good thing. They could admire the fact that nothing ever seems to faze them; it might seem as though they are incredibly robust.

Disconnected

What this could show is that these people are on the other end of the spectrum, meaning that they are controlled by their emotions, and one does their best to control how they feel and are in a very repressed state. Yet, while one side can be seen as being better than the other, they are both going to lead to problems.

Ultimately, they are going to spend a lot of time being out of touch with how they feel, and this is going to make it hard for people to deeply connect to them and for them to deeply connect to others. If they do get in touch with how they feel, it could be because they are by themselves.

What's going on?

Therefore, it is not that they don't have emotions; it is that they find it hard to express how they feel around others and don't have a strong connection with how they feel. So, even though they will come across as stoic around others, this could just be an act, and there could even be times when they are highly emotional when they are by themselves and during certain periods of their life.

When this is what feels safe, it is likely to show that they fear that something bad will happen if they embrace how they feel around others. If they were to get in touch with their body, they may find that they fear that they will be rejected and abandoned.

The Reason

During their younger years, they may have been brought up by a parent or parents' who were unable to be there for them emotionally. If they expressed their emotions around them, they may have been rejected and abandoned.

Through being treated in this way, they would have learnt that it wasn't safe for them to express their emotions. To survive, they would have had to disconnect from how they felt and create a false self.

Chapter 13

Self-Worth

Do You Believe That You Need To Be Good At Everything?

What is clear is that if someone wants to be good at something, they will need to put the work in and be patient. In addition to the time that they need to put in each week, there can be moments when they will need to change what they are doing.

The Next Level

Doing this will allow them to continue to grow, whereas if they were to do the same thing, this might not take place. This could mean that they will only need to make a few minor adjustments.

Then again, they may need to completely change what they are doing. For example, if they wanted to become a good martial artist, it could just be a case of changing their routine.

A Familiar Process

If they were to take a step back, they may find that there are a number of things that they are already good at. This could relate to things that they have done since they were very young.

But as they have been able to do these things for so long, they may find that they don't even think about them. It is then just part of who they are, and there is no reason for them to think about how their life used to be.

Feedback

Even so, there could be times when they come into contact with people who admire what they can do. Some of these people may respond in this way because they would also like to be able to do the same thing.

Perhaps they are working hard to be able to do what one can do, or it might be nothing more than a dream. Along with this, there are likely to be moments when they admire what other people can do.

A Balanced Outlook

But even when they do come into contact with people like this, it doesn't mean that they will feel inferior. One is then going to be in touch with their inherent value, and this means that they won't believe that their value is based on what they do.

As a result of this, it is going to be a lot easier for them to learn new things and to accept that it is not possible for them to be good at everything. So, if they do something and it takes a while for them to get the hang of it, there will be no need for them to punish themselves.

A Human Being

They are, after all, an imperfect human being, which means that it is going to be normal for them to get things wrong and to make mistakes from time to time. With this in mind, if they haven't done something before, there is going to be no reason for them to be good at it straight away.

Therefore, when it comes to learning something new, they will be able to be patient and talk to themselves in a positive manner. And, if they were to try something new but didn't want to continue, they could stop doing it without feeling like a failure.

Two Sides

Their inner dialogue is generally going to be supportive, and as this is the case, they are less likely to believe that other people will judge them. This comes down to the fact that what is taking place within them will not only have a big effect on how they expect other people to treat them, but also on how they treat them.

One could then try something and find it hard to get it right, but they won't be waiting for someone to criticise them, for instance. Through having self-compassion, they will treat themselves with love and respect.

Another Experience

However, although this is how some people will experience life, there are going to be others who are unable to relate to this. Deep down, someone like this can believe that they need to be good at everything.

Thus, even if they are not aware of what they believe, they will be aware of the effect that this has on their life. If they can't do something, they might do everything they can to hide this from others.

Avoidance

One of the ways that this could take place is by making sure that they avoid going to places where they would have to do the things that they can't do. As if they were to take place, they could end up feeling exposed.

What this can also do is cause them to work extremely hard whenever they try something new, which can allow them to make a lot of progress in a very short period of time. This will then be a way for them to minimise the amount of negative feedback that they believe they will receive.

Pressure

There is going to be how they feel when they try something new, and when they are around someone who can do something that they can't. Yet, even though these two situations are different, it doesn't mean that one will feel completely different.

The fact that they can't do something is likely to cause them to feel bad, and then they will probably feel even worse if they can't do it straight away. And as someone else can do something that they can't, this could cause them to feel as though they are inferior.

A Human Doing

If they were to take a step back and reflect on what is taking place, they may find that they feel worthless. Their value is then going to be attached to what they do as opposed to who they are.

As this is how they see themselves, it is going to be vital for them to do everything they can to hide this from others. This can cause them to create the impression that they are more-than-human.

Far Too Dangerous

If they were to reveal their true self, they are likely to believe that this would cause them to be rejected and/or abandoned. There is a strong chance that their early years were a time when their value was based on what they did and not on who they were.

Chapter 14

Self-Worth

Do You Only Feel Valuable When You Please Others?

It could be said that there are going to be times when it is possible to please others and times when it isn't. But while this is just part of life, it doesn't mean that everyone is able to accept this.

One Experience

When someone can accept this, it doesn't mean that they won't try to please others; it just means that it will be easier for them to handle the moments when it doesn't take place. Behind just about everything that they do could be the desire to gain other people's approval.

As a result of this, it is going to be a challenge for them to focus on their own needs, and this is going to create inner conflict. Still, the pain that they experience through neglecting themselves is likely to be kept in check.

Positive Feedback

The reason for this is that doing what they can to fulfil other people's needs will allow them to receive approval. What happens externally is generally going to keep what is taking place within them at bay.

When this doesn't happen, they could end up feeling down and depressed. If they are aware of the fact that they are living in an inauthentic manner, they will be able to understand why they feel this way.

The Solution

One could then look into what they can do to change their life and to live in a way that will allow them to fulfil their own needs. Alternatively, they might not believe that their mood has anything to do with their behaviour.

What may allow them to change their mood is to look into what they can do for someone else. The positive feedback that they receive from them might enable them to rise once more.

Another Experience

On the other hand, when someone is unable to accept that it is not always possible to please others, they can end up experiencing even more pain. Their whole life can end up being completely taken over by their need to do what other people want.

Their needs will be replaced by other people's needs, and one is going to be nothing more than an extension of others. As they are estranged from their true self, there will be a false self in its place.

The Same Outlook

Therefore, regardless of whether someone is able to accept that they can't always please others, they are still going to suffer. Also, by trying to please one person, it is going to cause them to displease someone else.

Ultimately, they are going to be playing a game that they can't win and, until they realise this, they are going to be creating unnecessary problems for themselves. Their life would be far more fulfilling if they were able to pay attention to their own needs.

Self-Worth

Yet, while paying attention to their own needs is going to allow them to live a life that is worth living, there is going to be a reason why they behave in this way. What they could find is that pleasing others allows them to feel good about themselves.

So, if they were to take a step back and focus on their own needs, they would end up feeling worthless. It is then not that they truly want to please others; it is that they don't want to feel bad about themselves.

An Unconscious Process

In general, this is likely to be something that just happens and not something that they even think about. Their need to feel good about themselves will be what drives their behaviour, and it could be said that this is perfectly normal.

It is then going to be vital for them to change what is taking place within them; if they don't, their behaviour will stay the same. Taking a step back and no longer trying to please others might be hard in the short-term, but it will be worth it in the long-term.

A Closer Look

What they are likely to find is that their value is attached to pleasing others, meaning that they are a human doing. Whereas if their value was based on who they are as opposed to what they do, they would truly be a human being.

This shows that they are out of touch with their inherent value, and this could be how their life has always been. If this is the case, it is likely to be due to what took place during their developmental years.

A Lack of Love

Their parent or parents' may have seen them as nothing more than an extension of themselves. This would have stopped them from being able to accept the fact that they had their own needs and feelings, and it would have caused them to develop a false self.

If they did what their parent or parents' wanted, they would have approved of them, which would have allowed them to feel good about themselves. But if one didn't do what they wanted, they may have been harmed and/or neglected.

Chapter 15

Self-Worth

Do You Believe That Your Value Is Defined By What You Do?

If someone were to go on holiday or take some time off work, it doesn't mean that they will be able to take it easy. This could be a time when their mind will be consumed with what is taking place back home.

There can be what they are not doing while they are away, and what they will need to do once they get back. So even though their body will be in another country, or another part of the country, their mind will be where it usually is.

One Option

Consequently, they might end up having to drink alcohol in order to take their mind off what is taking place back home. Yet even though this will settle them down, it is not going to last for very long.

Before long, they will soon have to face what is taking place in their mind, and it could end up being even worse. What this comes down to is that even though they will feel relaxed when they drink alcohol, it could be said that it is artificial relaxation.

Force

They are then forcing themselves to relax, and this shows that they are carrying a lot of tension within them. But as their mind is so busy, this could be seen as the only option that is available to them.

When they get back home, they might experience a sense of relief; this is because it will be possible for them to get things done. Being away will have caused them to experience a lot of stress, and they will then be glad that it is over.

Highly Motivated

What is also clear is that they have a lot of motivation. Something within them is going to be driving them forward; if they didn't have this drive, they wouldn't be able to behave in this way.

And no matter what this person achieves, it is not going to take away their motivation. One is then a human being, but they are going to act as though they are a machine - a machine that doesn't run out of fuel.

On Top Of the Mountain

Through having this drive and taking action, there is a chance that they have been able to elevate themselves to a certain position in their career. They might then have a lot of money and/or they could be perceived as being 'successful' by other people.

If what they do is held in high esteem by the society they live in, it is going to cause them to receive a lot of approval. Naturally, this is going to have a positive effect on their wellbeing.

Deep Fulfilment

When what they do is something that is in alignment with their own needs and values, the approval that they receive from others will be the icing on the cake. They are then not going to be doing what they do to please others.

Alternatively, what they do might not be very fulfilling, but it could be something that allows them to please a lot of people. This is then going to be like a cake without the filling; it is not going to be very satisfying.

A Closer Look

Nevertheless, even if they do come across as though they have it all together, it doesn't mean that this is the case. The reason why they are unable to relax can be due to the fact that they believe that their value is based on what they do as opposed to who they are.

Therefore, the only way they will be able to feel good about themselves is if they are doing something. They are then going to be a human being who has inherent value, but they are not going to realise this.

A Slave

They can then believe that they are only as good as the last thing that they have achieved, and even if they feel good after this, it is not going to last. It will then be vital for them to achieve something else.

Letting go is not going to be an option for them; if they were to do this, they would soon have to face up to how they feel about themselves. Ultimately, it is not going to matter what they achieve externally, as it won't have a lasting effect on what is taking place within them.

A Big Contrast

They are then going to achieve things that have value, but they are going to see themselves as someone who has no value. This could then cause them to wonder why they see themselves in this way.

As their value is based on who they are and not on what they do, it is likely to show that they didn't receive what they needed during their early years in order to develop in the right way.

Going Deeper

During this time, it is highly unlikely that they received unconditional love. The attention and approval that they received from their parent or parents' would have been the result of them playing a certain role.

So if one did what one or both of these people wanted, it would have allowed them to receive positive feedback. This would then have caused them to disconnect from their true self and stopped them from being able to connect to their inherent value and lovability.

Chapter 16

Sense of Self

Do You Feel Empty?

When someone feels like a whole human being, they are going to feel supported and be in tune with what is taking place in their head and what is going on in their body. They are then not going to be dead from the neck or the waist down.

Connected

As a result of this, they will be able to utilise the information that is within their body, meaning they won't need to rely on their mind. They will also typically be aware of how they feel and what their needs are.

It is therefore going to be a lot easier for them to fulfil their needs, which can enable them to live a fulfilling life. And through being aware of how they feel, they should also be able to express how they feel.

The Outcome

Due to this, there is a strong chance that they will have close connections with other people. The reason for this is that close connections are not formed through simply sharing ideas alone; they are generally formed through sharing what is taking place at a deeper level.

85

Thus, when one is able to express how they feel, it will allow other people to feel connected to them. Furthermore, how they feel around someone will tell them a lot about whether this person is a good influence on them.

Guidance

There will be the effect their intuition has, too, and this is going to provide them with instant information. At times, their mind might not know what is going on, and this could result in them ignoring their inner guidance.

But if they are in tune with themselves, this could be the exception as opposed to the rule. Their mind is the part of them that has largely been conditioned by the external world; whereas their inner guidance is the result of what is provided by their body - the seat of their true self - and what they are able to sense by automatically picking up on what is going on around them and at a distance, at an energetic level.

Full Up

One of the benefits of feeling like a whole human being is that they are not going to feel as though they need someone or something to complete them. Said another way, they are going to be an interdependent human being; they will need others, but they won't need one person in particular.

Now, this is not to say that there won't be moments when they will feel as though something is missing. When this happens, it could be a sign that they are going through a breakup or that someone has passed on, for instance.

Part of Life

However, after a certain amount of time has passed and they have been able to grieve, they should soon feel like a whole human being again. Life is not one big holiday, after all, and this is why it is going to be normal for them to feel as though they have been knocked over from time to time.

When they do get knocked down, they might end up being drawn to things that they wouldn't usually be drawn to. Perhaps they could drink more than they usually do, or eat the wrong kind of food, for instance.

A Different Reality

On the other hand, if someone doesn't feel whole, their experience on this planet is going to be very different. This may mean that it is normal for them to be drawn to things that are not good for them.

Alternatively, they could simply be drawn to one thing and not care about anything else. For example, they might find that they tend to drink a lot of alcohol or take drugs, or they might eat too much food or buy too much stuff.

A Black Hole

Deep down, they are likely to believe that this will allow them to finally feel like a whole human being. It is then as though the emptiness within them will be filled by consuming things from the external world.

Part of them might even realise that this is not working, but a stronger part of them that is in control might not be willing to face up to this. As far as this part of them is concerned, this could be the only way that it is going to take place.

Two Experiences

Yet, while they are going to feel numb and as though they are missing something, it doesn't mean that they will always feel this way. There could also be moments when they feel incredibly needy and emotionally raw.

It can seem as though they are either on top of a building looking down or as though they are trapped in a pool that is full of sludge. One is then either disconnected from their body and how they feel, or they are unable to think clearly and are practically drowning in how they feel.

The Trigger

What can cause them to go from one extreme to another is if they happen to end up in a relationship, and this comes to an end. They will have formed an attachment to someone, and as this attachment is broken, it will have caused them to experience the pain of loss and unlocked some of the pain that is within them.

It can be as if they don't need anything at one point in time, and at another, it can be as though they need everything. So, regardless of how developed their intellect may or may not be, what is clear is that they are emotionally underdeveloped.

A Closer Look

When someone experiences life in this way, it is highly likely that they didn't receive what they needed during their formative years, with them only experiencing a physical but not an emotional birth. The attunement that they needed, in order to grow and develop into a whole human being, probably wasn't provided on a consistent basis.

Chapter 17

Success

Are You An Overachiever?

When someone values themselves, they can do what it takes to achieve their goals. Quite simply, they are not going to be willing to settle in life, and this will play a part in what pushes them forward.

As a result of this, they could be in a position where they have achieved a number of their goals. Alternatively, they could be at the beginning of their life, and this means that they might not have achieved much at this point in time.

One Direction

Yet, regardless of what they have achieved so far, it is only going to be a matter of time before they are able to go to the next level. Now, this is not to say that everything will always go to plan.

There will be moments when they have setbacks, but that won't cause them to give up. The main reason for this is that when something goes wrong, they probably won't take it personally.

A Big Difference

This comes down to the fact that their value is going to be based on who they are, not on what they do. Therefore, when something goes wrong, it is not going to mean that there is something inherently wrong with them.

91

They will then be able to take a step back and look into what they can do to move forward. Whereas if they took it personally when something didn't go to plan, it would take them a while to get back on their feet again - that's if they don't give up altogether.

Resilience

It has been said that a big part of success is having the ability to keep going, no matter what happens. So, if someone doesn't have the tendency to throw the towel in, so to speak, when something doesn't go to plan, it will be a lot easier for them to move through the challenges that arise and achieve their goal.

And each time that they achieve something, it will give them even more belief in their own ability to achieve their goals. If their friends or family were asked to describe them, they might say that they have high self-esteem.

A Popular Term

This is often seen as a key element when it comes to being successful. Based on this outlook, someone is not going to get very far if they have low self-esteem.

When someone doesn't value themselves, then, they are not likely to get very far in life. If their life has only just begun, they might not believe that they will achieve a lot, and if they have been on this earth for quite some time, they might not have achieved much.

Just how It Is

If they were to come into contact with someone who is doing well in life, they might believe that they are different. This person is then going to have something that they themselves don't, which is why it is not possible for them to change their life.

Then again, they could be in touch with what is taking place at a deeper level, meaning they will be aware of the fact that they feel as though they don't deserve to experience life differently. They could then be good at certain things, but they won't allow themselves to take the next step.

Self-Sabotage

When it comes to their career, for instance, they might hold themselves back. If an opportunity were to arise, they might not take it, or they could end up being overwhelmed with anxiety and underperforming.

Conversely, they might not be aware of what is taking place within them, and this could cause them to believe that other people want to hold them back. It is then going to be normal for them to have moments when they feel like a victim, even if they don't have a victim mentality.

Black And White

If someone doesn't value themselves, there is only going to be one outcome. Consequently, it is going to be relatively easy to realise when someone is in a position where they don't feel good about themselves.

However, while it might seem as though this is the case, it is not always going to work this way. What can also happen is that someone can both consciously and unconsciously resist how they truly feel and end up using the pain within them as fuel.

Overachievers

Using the pain that is within them to drive them forward could allow them to become extremely successful. Once they get to a certain level, other people could see them as an example to follow.

Thus, how they are treated by others is going to be radically different to how they see themselves. The downside is that no matter what they achieve, it won't have much of an effect on them.

Avoidance

Their desire to achieve is going to be fuelled by their need to avoid how they feel, and this is why they are fighting a losing battle. After they have achieved something, it may allow them to feel better, yet after a little while, their true feelings will probably come to the surface again.

This could be something that they have experienced many times, but it doesn't mean that they will be able to take a step back and change their life. The only way that their life will truly change is if they let go of the pain that is within them.

Early Years

These feelings will be coming from their true self, and this part of them is going to be deeply wounded. When someone experiences life in this way, it can be due to what took place during their developmental years.

During this time, they are likely to have missed out on the love that they needed. Below their compulsion to achieve things, then, can be their repressed adult and unmet developmental need to be loved.

The Second Part

How To Reconnect To Your True Self

Chapter 18

The Power Of Letting Go

Now that you have read all of the chapters above, you may have found that you could relate to all of the examples or only some of them. But regardless of this, what will be clear is that you will no longer want to have a weak connection with or hide your true self.

This desire is going to play a vital role in your ability to transform your life. That's not to say that this desire will only have a positive effect on your life, though.

A Double-Edged Sword

The reason I say this is because the very thing that can help you move forward can be the very thing that holds you back and causes you to suffer even more. Out of your need to move forward, you can end up feeling frustrated and angry when things don't go as you would like them to.

Additionally, having such a strong need to change your life can push what you desire ever further out of your grasp. This is something that has been called the healing paradox.

Going Deeper

You may be wondering why having a strong need to change your life can push the change that you desire further out of your reach. To understand why this is, it will be necessary to take a closer look at the law of resonance.

This law states that everyone and everything is made up of vibrating energy (and this means that your sense of being separate from everyone and everything, something that allows you to have

99

your own experience, is an illusion) and, therefore, for someone to meet a certain person or have a certain experience, they will need to be vibrating at the right frequency. When it comes to what influences this frequency, it will be influenced by one's thoughts, emotions, feelings, beliefs, and trauma, among other things.

Two Levels

The universe, or whatever word you feel comfortable with, doesn't understand negation, and neither does your mind (to demonstrate this point, please don't imagine a purple dog). If you are in a place of frustration and desperation, for instance, that's where part of you will be at an energetic level.

The outcome of this is that you will attract and be attracted to people, situations, circumstances, and events that are an energetic match with this part, as well as other parts, of you. What this demonstrates is how powerful you are and how important it is for you to realise that needing your life to change, actually makes it harder for you to do this.

A Few Quotes

Carl Jung once said that "what you resist not only persists, but will grow in size." Dov Baron, one of my first mentors, often said something like: You can have anything you want as long as you are not attached to it.

This shows how important it is not to be strongly attached to an outcome and why it is incredibly important to see this as a journey, as opposed to a destination. Right now, as a result of how much pain you are in and how unfulfilling your life is, you might not be able to let go, but this will change as long as you do the inner work.

The Other Part

As for the power of your feelings, this doesn't mean that you need to deny how you feel and always be positive. This is simply something for you to keep in mind when you do experience a strong need for your life to change.

If you deny how you feel, you would be in a place of resistance, and the feelings that you push out of your conscious mind would still affect your reality. Furthermore, denying how you feel is not going to help you build a stronger connection with your true self.

Chapter 19

A Unique Path

This kind of work is not linear, so there can be moments when it seems like you are going backwards, not forward. Being able to trust in your journey and that you will find what you need when you need it is the key.

Paying attention to what you were like when you took your first step on this journey and the gradual changes that you make along the way will make it easier for you to keep going. Also, it doesn't matter what kind of progress other people appear to be making, as they have their own journeys.

You are a valuable human being who is on a journey that needs to be honoured. Naturally, if you compare where you are with where you started, you will be able to more accurately gauge the progress you are making.

A Key Point

For example, even if you were to compare your life with another person who is the same age as you or a similar age, it doesn't mean that you had the same start to life as they did. To use an analogy, it could be as though they started a few miles ahead of you, at least in some respects.

But, as you are on your own path, and so is everyone else, you are not here to compare your life with another's or to live another person's version of how life should be lived. What the above example illustrates is that while it can be normal for your mind to automatically compare your life with the lives of others, it doesn't mean that you need to get caught up with and identify with these comparisons.

103

Chapter 20

The Body And The Mind

In order for you to gradually build a stronger connection with and reveal your true self, or to no longer have so many moments when you hide yourself, it is going to be essential for you to feel safe enough to do so. And when it comes to feeling safe, it is more about the body than it is about the mind.

The mind can believe just about anything, but if the body doesn't feel safe enough to fulfil what the mind believes, not a lot is likely to happen. The trouble is that in our emotionally repressed, disconnected, and mind-centric society, a lot of attention is given to the mind and to thoughts while the body and feelings are largely overlooked (the body is then merely there to support the head or intellect, doesn't possess wisdom, and has about as much to do with inner change as a jelly does to the formation of a cloud).

A Thing Of The Past

It is then as if, as society has become more technological, the body and feelings are no longer seen as being important and have been left behind, whilst the mind/intellect and thoughts have been exalted to a god-like status. Due to this, the emotional self typically has very little importance and, like a wild animal, needs to be dominated and controlled by the mind.

This can also be seen as an example of how the masculine element has been elevated and the feminine element has been lowered and is even seen as being inferior. Willpower and force are then held in high esteem, and letting go and surrendering – that's if these qualities are even mentioned – have become masculinised, with both often being seen as something that takes place through force.

105

The Tip Of The Iceberg

This collective lack of outer (mind and body) and inner (thoughts, feelings, and instincts) integration (something that could be seen as a collective lack of integration between the masculine and feminine elements) has led to the commonly held view that, when it comes to change and transformation, it's mainly about changing one's thoughts and the creation of a multitude of therapies that are focused purely on achieving this aim. Another part of this is that it is often as if someone begins and ends with their conscious mind and doesn't even have an unconscious mind.

Or, if this part of someone is mentioned, it is likely to be seen as something that can simply be 'reprogrammed' with positive thoughts and beliefs, for instance. When this happens, what is going on outside of their conscious awareness is not going to be explored.

A Dark Side

Naturally, this has and will continue to lead to a lot of 'negativity' building up inside the average person's unconscious mind and the collective unconscious. Yet, as this material is largely overlooked, this inner 'darkness' ends up being externalised in some shape or form at a local and global level, but as the connection between the inner and the outer is not made, at least in mainstream society, not a great deal is likely to change.

Badness is then something that is always 'out there' and needs to be defeated as opposed to something that is a reflection of what is going on internally that needs to be acknowledged and resolved. Unsurprisingly, certain situations, circumstances, and events are repeated, time and time again.

The Elephant in the Room

And, as repressed pain is rarely, if ever, acknowledged, it means that the impact that it can have on someone's mental, emotional, and physical health and on how they behave is also largely overlooked. The fact that it is rarely mentioned surely shows how effective the average person's brain is at repressing pain (and when it comes to how effective it is at doing this, it can depend on how much pain they are carrying and how nurturing their developmental years were and what it was like for them in their mother's womb).

If this were something that was widely understood, there wouldn't be such a strong emphasis on the mind, and what is going on at a deeper level would be explored. As things stand, it is often as though someone was born with a fully formed frontal cortex and experienced 'negative' thoughts and beliefs from this moment onwards and the pain that they experienced at the beginning of their life, that's if it is even mentioned, was also the result of their thinking and has just disappeared.

A New Ability

But, while an adult can unknowingly (as they may have come to believe that their thoughts always create their feelings) use their thinking brain to repress how they feel by having certain thoughts, beliefs, and ideas, and deceiving themselves in the process; they wouldn't have been able to do this very early on. This part of them was underdeveloped (this is why it is possible to have a well-developed intellect and be emotionally stunted as an adult as the former develops later) and they would have had to rely on their brain responding in a certain way and their body shutting down to keep their pain out of their conscious awareness.

With this understanding, using a mind-based approach to deal with the impact that their early experiences had on them will be similar to cutting the top off a weed and believing that it has now been removed. Needless to say, the root will still be there, and for it to be removed, a different approach will be needed.

An Analogy

Another way to understand this would be to imagine that a wall is starting to collapse as the foundations are weak. To resolve what is going on, it will be necessary to not only fix the wall but also fix the foundations.

However, for whatever reason, the person who is fixing the wall doesn't even think about the foundations. let alone see them as being important, so the focus is on fixing the wall. By virtue of this, not only is one part being ignored, but a part that came after the first part will be used to repair a part that came before it.

The Eyes of an Adult

Finally, the general view that adults are thinking beings that feel, not feeling beings that think, can also be seen as a natural consequence of how an adult typically experiences life. A child has an experience that is more emotional in nature, while an adult typically has an experience that is more mental in nature.

An adult, then, by having a more mental experience of life and being far away from their early emotional experience of it, is not going to see a mind-based approach as missing anything. Yet, an emotional approach, even though they are first and foremost emotional beings, will be seen as missing the most important element – the mind.

Back To You

Let's pretend, for a moment, that you are depressed because you are carrying a lot of repressed pain, and this is the result of early deprivation. But, this is not something that you are aware of (you might have had this experience).

You reach out for the support of a therapist and end up being told that your 'negative' thoughts and beliefs are the problem and/or that you have a chemical imbalance (that's not to say that your brain chemicals don't play a part in your mental and emotional health), perhaps by someone who is also out of touch with their true self and is living on the surface of themselves. And, naturally, if someone is out of touch with their true self, they are not going to suggest that you connect to your own, let alone guide you through this process.

Ahistorical

What took place in your past and your unconscious mind is also not going to be explored, with what is going on in the present moment and your conscious mind being the point of focus. You could be told that your past is in the past, and so there is no need to focus on it, even though there is only the now moment, which means that your emotional baggage is not in the past; you are carrying it around with you.

Now, solely changing your thoughts and beliefs and even your behaviour might patch you up and allow you to function again, but it almost certainly won't allow you to reconnect to yourself and become more integrated; your false self and the defences that keep it in place will have just been strengthened.

A Bigger Gap

By strengthening your defences and even building more, you will end up being even more estranged from yourself. But, as you are not aware of the fact that you are suffering because the pain you are carrying is weighing you down, there will be no reason for you to question this approach.

As you will live in a mind-centric society, and the approach that was put forward to you will be an outgrowth of this, why would it enter your mind that you are carrying pain? The input that was trying to break through to your conscious mind and was making your life harder to handle will be kept at bay, at least in the short-term, allowing you to carry on as normal.

A Positive Impact

Furthermore, it is unlikely that using your frontal cortex to strengthen your defences and build more and changing your behaviour, will be the only things that will have allowed you to function again. What this wouldn't take into account is the impact that transference is likely to have had on the progress you have made.

In other words, at a conscious level, it would have been clear that this person wasn't your mother or father, but, at a deeper level, you wouldn't have realised this. Spending time with someone that was focused on you and was kind and caring would have had a positive effect on your wellbeing - as you are an interdependent human being that needs to be seen and heard - and allowed the underdeveloped parts of you, the parts that have no sense of time and are unable to see clearly, to believe that they were finally receiving the love that they missed out on.

Symbolic Love

But, as this stage of your life is over, it also means that these unmet developmental needs can't be met. The impact that their presence had on you will then gradually wear off, causing you to feel unloved and, perhaps, to end up being depressed again before long.

If this mind-based approach only allows you to carry on as normal in the short term, it will be clear why. You could then work with a therapist like this for decades and not make any real progress.

A Similar Scenario

Or, if you don't work with a therapist, you could end up going on a weekend course or a week-long retreat, with this being a time when you will use different mind-based techniques and perhaps some yoga and different 'spiritual' methods, but don't do any feeling work. You would still be engaging in transference with your facilitators and fellow students.

Once again, you could feel great during and for a little while after, and then, seemingly, out of nowhere, you could feel even worse than before. You would have unwittingly been caught up in an illusion and, as time passed, been forced to face reality.

Self-Sustaining

Irrespective of whether a mind-based and/or a 'spiritual' approach is used to keep your pain at bay, it will also help you to keep the wheels of society turning. In the same way that your false self will do what it can to keep your true self at bay and stop you from being real, the society that you live in is likely to do the same thing.

If you were to reconnect to yourself and your feelings, it would probably be a lot harder for you to not only behave in the same way but also to tolerate some of the things that take place at a local and national level. You would then be a threat to the dysfunctional system that is in place.

Beyond The Surface

Moreover, by purely focusing on what is going on up top, your consciousness won't really change, and this will prevent you from being able to radically change your life. And, as what is taking place inside you hasn't really changed and has just been pushed down and covered up, what is inside you is still going to be feeding into the collective consciousness and having an impact on what takes place on the planet as a whole.

When it comes to the collective consciousness, this can be seen as a field that holds what is taking place for humanity at both a conscious and unconscious level. From the level of the unphysical, it shapes what takes place in the physical world.

Real Change

Dealing with what is taking place for you at a deeper level and not just being patched up will serve you and the planet as a whole. You are then focusing on yourself by doing this work and are being 'selfish', but it will serve the rest of humanity.

This also illustrates that changing what is going on 'out there' is not the only way to change the world. And, if what is going on externally reflects what is going on internally for humanity as a whole, if what is going on internally is not changed, changing what is going on externally is likely to be nothing more than a temporary solution.

Chapter 21

The First Step

When it comes to your mind, it will be important for you to develop the ability to observe your inner world, and this ability can be developed by meditating. This can then play a big part in allowing you to no longer be controlled by your mind, and you can start to choose thoughts that are empowering and talk to yourself differently.

A positive inner dialogue will have an effect on how you see yourself, how you behave, and what you achieve. This observer self will also play a key role in you being able to work through your emotional wounds, with this being a time when you will be using both your observer (left brain) and experiencing self (right brain).

One Option

When it comes to meditating, this is not something that you have to do for an hour each day. To begin with, if you don't do this already, you can start by doing this for about ten minutes a few times a week.

By meditating for only a short amount of time and not very often, in the beginning, it is less likely to be seen as something that you have to do. As a result of this, you are more likely to both do it and keep doing it.

It's not a panacea

Before I go into how you can meditate, I think it's important to point out a few things. Meditation or mindfulness is often seen as a cureall in today's world, but it is not always beneficial.

If you are not in a good way, you may find that simply being with what is going on inside you is overwhelming, and if you are not in this position, you may find that engaging in this practice makes it harder for you to connect to how you feel. Taking this into account, it will be important for you to monitor how you get on and to stop if you notice that it is having a negative impact on you.

One Last Point

It has been said that one thing that meditation does is make the prefrontal cortex thicker. This is the part of the brain that manages higher-order functioning (one thing it is said to do is to regulate thoughts, emotions, and behaviour).

From this, it could be said that one of the reasons why meditation can improve someone's mental health and allow them to be more settled is because it aids in repression. To use an analogy, it will be like someone who lives in a room that is above a very noisy basement, but after soundproofing their room, it is now a lot quieter.

It hasn't disappeared

If they were to leave their soundproofed room, they would soon find out that the noise is still there. Likewise, if someone were to reconnect to what is taking place on the other side of their pre-frontal cortex, after having solely meditating for however long and overlooking the material that is held at a deeper level, they are also likely to see that not every part of them is at ease.

A calm mind is then not necessarily a sign that every part of one's being is calm. This is then similar to how a local anaesthetic can stop someone from being consciously aware of the pain that they are experiencing in a certain area of their body during an operation, but at a deeper level, they are still in pain.

114

A Natural Outcome

It would then make sense as to why, if someone meditates for a number of hours each day and does this for a long period of time, for example, they will end up finding it hard to connect to how they feel. Instead of becoming more connected to themselves, they will become more disconnected.

Their ability to reflect and see things clearly can be very good, but their ability to deeply connect with themselves and others will have been undermined. In other words, they will have become out of balance.

A Simple Method

Anyway, first, you can find somewhere that is quiet and where you can sit with your back upright, and you may find that listening to relaxing meditation music helps. After this, it will be a time when you will focus on your breathing and simply watch what is taking place inside you; neither trying to change nor resist what is going on.

If this option is too passive for you, what you could do is go for a walk in nature or a wooded area and focus on your breathing and observe your inner processes there. This might seem more natural and less like something that you have to do.

Nature

Simply spending time in nature, without the intention of meditating, may allow you to be more at ease. A woodland or field can be the perfect place for this.

When you are somewhere that is quiet, it can also help you to reconnect with yourself. If you have your smartphone with you, it will probably be best to make sure that it is on silent so that you won't be disturbed.

Going Further

By having no external distractions to consume your attention, you will be able to be with yourself. There might be moments when you come into contact with inner material that makes you feel uncomfortable, and moments when this doesn't happen and you feel comfortable.

Taking your footwear and socks off and walking around barefoot can also help you reconnect with yourself. As strange as this may sound to you right now, touching or hugging a tree is another thing that you could do.

Chapter 22

The Second Step

If you have already developed the ability to meditate, you might be ready to go to the next stage. This can be seen as the emotional level, and what is taking place in your body.

Here, it will relate to facing the pain that was too much for you to handle and integrate and had to be repressed during your early years and experiencing your unmet developmental needs. Getting in touch with the pain in your body and crying out this pain is one way to go about doing this, and this can involve connecting to your inner child or inner children, as there are likely to be many child parts inside you.

Many Parts

One thing that early trauma does - any trauma for that matter - in addition to creating an inner disconnection, is a state of being fractured. So, when you experienced something during your early years that was overwhelming and too much for your system to face and integrate, this would have been a time when part of your consciousness was split-off and repressed, and this may have been something that took place hundreds, if not thousands, of times.

On one side, this would have allowed you to keep it together and function, but on the other side, it would have weakened you and created a divide between your mind and body. After a while, this part of you would have been out of your reach, and some of your energy would have been used then and will continue to be used now, to keep the pain in this part of you out of your conscious awareness.

One Purpose

What this illustrates is how your brain is designed to keep you unconscious - unaware of what is taking place inside you. It doesn't do this to harm you; it does this to keep you alive.

The other part of this is that it does this so that you can pass on your genes. If you didn't have the ability to repress pain, you wouldn't be able to keep it together and function. This would probably mean that you wouldn't be able to pass on your genes.

The Monkey Body

But, while this pain will be repressed, along with the unmet needs that go with it, it can cause your mind to play up. This can result in you having automatic and 'negative' thoughts, faulty perceptions, phobias, irrational feelings, obsessions, compulsions and nightmares.

Without this understanding, it will be normal for your mind or 'ego' to be seen as the problem. With this understanding, what is taking place in your mind can be seen as providing valuable feedback about what is taking place at a deeper level.

An Analogy

When this part of you is seen as the problem and steps are taken to deal with what is taking place at this level, it will be the equivalent of killing the messenger. The mind, as would be the case when someone shares an important message, is then blamed and silenced.

When it simply has a message to share and is not at fault for what is being expressed. Also, just as when a messenger is killed, silencing your mind won't change anything.

Recycling The Past

And, you may find, as time goes by, that most of what you fear relates to things that have already happened. For example, you may have a fear of dying, being abandoned and/or being harmed.

But, as your brain has blocked out these early experiences to protect you, your conscious mind will believe that what you fear is about to happen, not something that has already happened. This shows how your brain is having an effect on how you see reality and why it has been said that we see with our brains, not our eyes.

Repeating The Past

Now, this doesn't mean that it is not possible for you to recreate your early experiences. This is something that you might be able to relate to, with you having moments in your life when something happened and you felt like you were going to die, were left and/or were harmed.

These are experiences that you are likely to have unconsciously manifested, which means that you won't have consciously chosen to have these experiences. Along with what your brain will project onto reality, then, will be the impact that your own consciousness is having on how you experience life itself.

Watered Down

Anyway, without access to most, let alone all of your consciousness, you won't be the person you could be. When you are connecting to these parts, parts that can relate to when you were a child, infant, and toddler, and feel the pain and experience the needs that were not met all those years ago, you will gradually be reclaiming all of yourself.

You are likely to see that, although you are now an adult, when you engage in this work, it is as though you have gone back in time. This will show you that time alone won't have allowed you to move on and that your emotional wounds have been frozen in time.

It's Different

If you didn't understand that you are simply connecting to undeveloped parts of yourself, you might think that you were regressing. How you feel would then be a defence against pain, not a sign that you are facing your pain.

In reality, a part of yourself that has been inside of you for however long will have entered your conscious awareness. Therefore, you won't have reverted to an earlier stage of your life; you will have just connected to what is taking place inside you.

External Support

Assuming that you haven't engaged in this work before, what you may need to do is to reach out for external support. If you don't feel comfortable connecting to how you feel, working with a therapist or healer at this time will be a good idea.

By being in the presence of someone like this, you will be able to go where you wouldn't ordinarily go by yourself. In other words, they will be holding the space for you until you can hold it for yourself.

The Right Choice

You may not have a preference when it comes to whether you work with a man or a woman. Then again, you may prefer to work with a man/woman as this will make it easier for you to relax and gradually open up.

If you were deeply wounded by your father or another male family member, or your mother or another female family member, this is to be expected. Of course, a male/female therapist/healer won't be your father/mother or another family member, but thanks to transference, where a part of you will automatically see them in this way, it won't matter as an old face will be placed onto a new face, so to speak.

It's Normal

Still, once you have found someone who you feel comfortable with you are still going to be engaging in transference. Along with what they are actually like, projecting into them someone from your past who you felt comfortable with is also likely to play a part in why you feel comfortable with them.

This shows that transference is neutral; whether it has a positive or negative effect will mainly depend on whether it is or isn't acknowledged and what happens after. Ultimately, it can be seen as something that takes place to help you become aware of what needs to be resolved within you and assist in you becoming a more integrated and whole human being.

Reconnecting

Irrespective of whether you do or don't reach out for support, when you engage in this work, it will be a good idea for you to find somewhere quiet, where you can relax and feel safe. Next, you can either sit down with your back upright or lie on your back on your bed.

From here, you can put your hands on your chest as this can make it easier for you to connect to how you feel (putting your hands on your sacral can also help as this is another emotional centre) or on either side of your hips as this can make it easier for you to feel safe and be more connected to your body. Another thing that can allow you to connect to your body and how you feel is to listen to relaxing music, hold an old teddy bear (or a new one) and look at pictures of yourself from your early years.

No Rush

You may find that you soon start to connect to a split-off part, with this being a time when a visual memory and the sensations, feelings, and needs that go with it enter your conscious awareness (or there might not be a visual memory and you might only connect to sensations, feelings, and needs). Before long, you can be crying out pain and connecting to and experiencing the needs that were not met.

As this type of work is not linear, you can feel worse before you feel better, and as you are likely to carry many, many layers of pain inside you, it can seem, at times, as though you are going over the same wounds and are not making progress. The key is to keep going, and as time passes, you are likely to see that you are making progress.

A Crucial Point

And, as you are reconnecting to and experiencing feelings from your early years, it means that you are not simply expressing feelings that relate to your adult life. Now, that's not to say connecting to how you feel about something in your adult life won't provide a starting point and allow you to gradually go deeper inside yourself.

But, if you were to only express feelings that relate to what is going on in the here and now and not the feelings that relate to your developmental years, you are unlikely to heal anything. At best, you might feel more settled as tension has been released (just as you are likely to feel more settled after you have been running, cycling, or dancing, for instance, as tension, along with pain killing endorphins, will have been released) but, as you have not reconnected to and experienced what is going on at a deeper level, it probably wouldn't be long until your inner experience goes back to how it was before and your life is unlikely to truly change either.

Inner Fire

This is why getting angry about something and/or someone from your past and hitting something is unlikely to resolve anything. Once again, you might feel more settled thanks to letting go of tension, but that will be about it.

If, however, you were to use this anger to reconnect to the anger that you experienced during your younger years when a need or a number of needs were not met and experienced the hurt that is likely to be underneath it, over time, you would probably carry around less anger. This is why it is so important for you to experience your feelings in their original context, as that's what heals.

Another Example

The same applies to anxiety inasmuch as purely focusing on and trying to remove it is unlikely to resolve anything. Just as with anger, there can be what is going on at a deeper level that needs to be acknowledged and worked through.

Ergo, if you find that you often experience anxiety, below this can be unresolved wounds that relate to when you were harmed and/or left and were totally powerless, for instance. In this case, the anxiety that you experience will be the result of what your unconscious mind is projecting onto the present and has no relevance to the present moment.

The Past Is Present

Your system will then be preparing you for a threat that has long passed. But, as the impact of what took place has not been resolved, what has already happened is continually seen as something that is about to happen.

Using an approach that purely focuses on anxiety (a symptom), then, is going to mean that what is going on below is not explored. The outcome of this is that your conscious mind can settle down, but the rest of you can still be full of tension (this is then akin to how positive thinking and affirmations can allow you to develop a 'positive mindset', but to have a body that is full of 'negativity').

It can't be forced

Working through all or even most of the pain that is inside you in one go might sound appealing. But, if this were to happen, it would be too much for you to handle, and you wouldn't be able to work through anything.

In general, pain will enter your conscious awareness when you are ready and strong enough to handle it. Trust that you will face what you need to face when you are ready to face it.

Totally Worn Out

Furthermore, when you are doing this work, it might not be long before you feel exhausted and can't go any further. This will show that your system has had enough for a little while, if not for the day.

As you get stronger and have worked through more layers, you might be able to engage in this process for longer. The main point here is that if you do shut down during this time and feel very tired, it will be best for you to take a break and not force yourself to continue.

An Essential Element

And, while you are feeling your pain, what is also likely to help is for you to breathe deeply. Currently, you may find that you typically breathe from your chest, not your stomach.

This will limit how much air you can take in, but it will also protect you from coming into contact with a lot of the pain that is locked deep inside you. So, by breathing from your stomach and not your chest, it can make it easier for you to connect with how you feel and experience deeper healing.

Unmet Needs

In case you are not sure about what is meant by connecting to and experiencing the needs that were not met during your developmental years, I will go into greater detail. Let's assume that you go into a memory of where you were left as a child.

This can be a time when you will feel unwanted, alone, and unloved. In this situation, you will probably have the need to be wanted, held, and loved.

Different Needs

If you were to connect to another inner experience, you might find that you have the need to be protected, held, and loved. There can then be certain needs that you continually connect to and needs that you don't always experience.

What will play a part in this is how old you are and what the context is. The needs that appear, though, will relate to needs that needed to be met.

Endless Insights

A by-product of doing this type of work is that during and after you have worked through some pain and expressed certain needs, you might understand why you behave in a particular way and/or why an area of your life is the way that it is. By connecting to the feelings and needs that have underpinned whatever has been going on, you will be able to join the dots, so to speak.

It will be as though you have been walking around in the dark, and now the lights are coming on. You won't need anyone else to shed light on why you behave in a certain way or why an area of your life is the way that it is, as the answers will be within you.

A Time of Surrender

As you are embracing what is going on within you, you won't be coming from a place of resistance. Of course, you will want your life to change, but having this need and trying to change how you feel is radically different.

Unlike mind-based approaches, you won't be trying to change, remove, fix or repair anything. You will simply be surrendering to what is going on within you.

From One Side to Another

And, it is by surrendering to the feeling of being unloved, unwanted, worthless, and afraid, for example, that you will be able to feel loved (and let love in), wanted, of worth, and brave. You are then embracing the feelings on the 'negative' side of the emotional spectrum to be able to naturally experience the feelings on the 'positive' side of the emotional spectrum.

Yet, as there are likely to be layers and layers of these feelings inside you, as a result of having numerous experiences where you felt this way, it won't just be a case of feeling unloved, unwanted, and worthless once, and that's the end of it. With that aside, this illustrates why letting go of what doesn't belong to you, not adding things, is the way for you to truly change how you feel.

It Doesn't End There

It is also through facing the split-off parts inside you that you will gradually become more whole and integrated. Also, facing the pain and experiencing the unmet developmental needs of your infant, toddler and child parts will allow you to gradually feel more like a strong and capable adult.

These are then two more examples of how surrendering to what is going on on one side of the spectrum will allow you to slowly move to the other side of it. In all of these cases, you are transmuting one expression into another.

An Additional Option

What can also play a part in you being able to let go of the pain and unmet developmental needs that are inside you is to write letters to your parent or parent's and whoever has wounded you over the years. During this time, you can write about whatever is on your mind and how you feel.

This approach is ideal if you can't get through to someone who is alive, and if the person who wounded you is no longer alive. Once you have written a letter, you can burn it.

The Other Side

Writing a letter that you would like to read from someone who has wounded you is another thing you can do. This can be a letter where they acknowledge what they put you through and express remorse.

It can be seen as the letter that they would write if they were mentally and emotionally healthy or alive. When you write this letter and then read it back to yourself, you can end up crying out a lot of pain.

The Same Impact

While you will have written it yourself, at an emotional level, you won't realise this. This is fortunate, as this might be the only way that you are able to receive this response.

By doing this, you are then taking matters into your own hands and not waiting for someone who is perhaps totally unavailable, if not long gone, to liberate you. The power will be in your own hands.

Creating Space

And, as you let go of your need to receive the love that you missed out on from your parent or parents' during your developmental years, you will be able to receive the love that is available. To use an analogy, it will be as if you have been going to a supermarket for years that usually has empty shelves and is malnourished as a result.

But, you gradually start to lose interest in going to this supermarket and end up going to another supermarket instead, and this one actually has food. The main difference is that you will be emotionally malnourished by looking for things that can't be provided by people who can't provide them.

A Gradual Acceptance

I want to make it clear, though, that it is unlikely to just be a case of you accepting the reality that your unmet developmental needs won't be met and that's it, as this is likely to be something that you will need to do many times throughout your healing journey. Once you have accepted this, you are likely to find that you soon notice that this is not something that every part of you fully accepts, as you are still behaving in a way that demonstrates that parts of you don't truly know this.

You will then have been awake at one point and asleep at another, and this can be seen as a normal part of letting go of your struggle for the love that was not available when you were growing up. This shows that accepting reality is a process and something that more of you will be able to accept as time passes, providing you continue to do the inner work.

Chapter 23

The Third Step

You might find that you are unable to connect to how you feel, or that you soon shut down and go into a collapsed state. If so, this may show that you are too frozen, constricted, armoured (look into Reichian character structures to find out more about body armouring and the pain that this allows someone to keep out of their conscious awareness), and don't feel safe enough to embrace how you feel at this moment in time.

Changing what is taking place in your mind is unlikely to have much of an effect on this. But if you have tried to settle down and feel safe by focusing on your mind, this will be something you have known on some level for a little while.

A Massive Impact

Being in a frozen, constricted and armoured state, along with having the need to run, fight, or just dissociate for no apparent reason, will be due to the impact that your early and perhaps adult experiences have had on your mind, brain, and body. Expecting your mind, brain, and body not to respond in this way, all the time you are carrying so much arousal and pain, would be similar to expecting a car to run without fuel; it's not going to happen.

The good news is that this arousal can be released - and as I've said above, the pain can be cried and written out - the bad news, if it is indeed bad news, is that it won't happen overnight. Yet, if you have experienced years of trauma, this is to be expected.

Cause and Effect

Carrying this arousal around is likely to be putting an enormous amount of pressure on your mind, brain, and body. Not feeling safe to express who you are is one of the effects.

Not feeling safe will then lead to a number of different symptoms, some of which I have touched upon above. Being emotionally settled is also going to be more or less impossible, that is, of course, if you don't have the tendency to be in a repressed, shut down and unfeeling state and you typically feel numb from the neck down or waist down, and there will be the effect that it has on your memory, ability to concentrate, be discerning and be present.

Moving Forward

With this in mind, if you have the tendency to be emotionally unsettled (a sign that your sympathetic nervous system will often be activated), you may find that you need to settle down before you can do any of the emotional work. Or, if your body does have the tendency to shut down and you can't feel (a sign that your parasympathetic nervous system will often be activated), you will need to loosen up before this can take place.

Once this starts to take place and your system becomes more open, you will be able to cry and write out the pain and hurt that is inside you (and it will also gradually get easier for you to take life in and receive). When it comes to finding a way to release this arousal or charge, the ideal will be for you to do this by yourself, without needing to rely on anyone else.

One Powerful Tool

What can allow you to be your own authority and play a big part in your own healing is something called Total Release Experience®, or TRE for short. This is a physical exercise that will allow you to release your trauma.

Your body will twitch, shake, and tremor, which is what animals do to release stress. There is a muscle group that connects our upper and lower body known as the psoas, and this muscle – as well as others – contracts when we experience a traumatic event. In this practice, you will learn to initiate your body's innate ability to tremor and hence release held tensions and symptoms of stress and anxiety from trauma.

The Next Step

In order for you to be able to use this technique, you would be advised to undergo the right training and get guidance from an authorised TRE UK® practitioner. Fortunately, it is relatively inexpensive to learn TRE, and after the second session, you will be able to practice at home.

This is a self-help, self-regulating practice that can save you thousands of pounds while also completely transforming your life. You will be utilising your body's natural ability to heal, and you will gradually become more resilient as time goes by, as long as you practice regularly.

Additional Support

If you engage in this kind of work, you may find that you need more emotional support than usual. Then again, you might notice that it doesn't take you long to feel better.

In this case, it might not be long until you need less support, not more. The support you do need could be provided by your friends or family, or you may use the assistance of your TRE UK® practitioner or a therapist, for instance.

Another Tool

Something called The Havening Technique can allow you to settle yourself down, too. This has been described as a method that has been designed to change the brain so that the memory is de-traumatized and its negative effects are removed from both the psyche and the body.

What is also part of the practice is something called Havening Touch®. This is, ultimately, where the sensory input of human touch is used as a therapeutic tool.

Two Choices

As with TRE, this is something that you can experience with the assistance of a certified Havening Techniques practitioner or by yourself. There are numerous videos online that will guide you through this process.

Whether you work with a certified practitioner or try this by yourself can depend on what is going on for you. Working with someone might be the best option at this stage of your journey if you are not in a good way right now.

Two More Options

Another technique that you can use to heal your trauma is Somatic Experiencing, with this being something that is relatively easy to learn. You might prefer this to the other techniques, or you may want to use all of them.

Neurofeedback brain training is another thing that you can use to settle yourself down. This is something that can be very powerful, but the drawback is that it is not cheap, and it might not even last.

One More

Along with these tools, what can also help you to settle down and reconnect to yourself is a form of bodywork called Bowen therapy, or the Bowen technique. During a Bowen session, the therapist will use their fingers or thumbs to move over muscle, ligament, tendon, and fascia in various parts of your body.

This will help your body to balance, repair, and reset itself. At some stage in the session, the therapist is likely to leave the room for a little while as this gives your body the chance to adapt to the treatment, and each session lasts between thirty minutes and one hour.

Loosening Up

One thing that developmental trauma would have done, trauma from any period of your life, in fact, is cause your fascia to tighten up. Your fascia is a sheet of connective tissue beneath your skin that surrounds and holds muscles and other organs.

Old memories and emotions will be held in this part of you (your feelings are also stored in your muscles, organs, and skin), which means that loosening up your fascia will allow you to let go of old pain and settle down your nervous system, which will allow you to develop a better connection with your body. Another thing it can do is loosen up your diaphragm, with this part of the body being seen as creating a barrier between the conscious and unconscious mind, and thoughts and feelings – in other words, it will separate you from a large part of your consciousness.

Coming Back Down

Another thing that you can do is practice something like Yoga, Tai Chi or Chi Gong. What these techniques can do is help bring you back into your body, release trauma, and develop a felt sense of safety and security.

These techniques can be learned by watching videos online or with the assistance of a professional teacher, who will guide you and make sure that you are performing each movement correctly. Undoubtedly, you don't want to injure yourself, but you may also not have the means, at this time, to seek professional guidance.

Chapter 24

The Importance Of Touch

Something that the late Conrad W Baars talked about in his work on emotional deprivation and how an emotional birth doesn't always take place, although a physical birth always does, is how important affirmation and human touch are when it comes to emotional development and the formation of a sense of self. The late Arthur Janov also spoke about how important it is for an infant to be held, caressed, and looked at to be able to develop in the right way.

Considering this, as well as the work that you do that relates to letting go, there will be what you need to receive. If you work with a therapist or healer, this will be a time when you will be able to be affirmed.

It Could Be Too Late

As for the touch that will allow you to grow, this can be provided through having a tantric massage. Or at the very least, the touch that will give you a sense of what you missed out on, providing you with a new reference point of how you can feel, and will unlock the pain of not being touched and the unmet developmental needs that go with it.

The reason why it might only allow the latter to take place and not the former is that, as you are no longer an infant, toddler, or child, it could be argued that it is too late for you to receive the touch that you missed out on. If it is too late, merely being touched and not working through the pain of not being touched and experiencing the unmet developmental needs that go with it will only allow you to momentarily feel better.

Another Consequence

As the human touch is a key part of what leads to the formation of a sense of self, it means that it also plays a part in what allows boundaries to be formed. When a baby is born, they have no sense of where they begin and end and where others begin and end and haven't developed a felt sense of safety and security or anything else for that matter.

This is why they can feel exposed and deeply vulnerable without clothes on, for instance. Being touched and held will play a part in what will allow them to develop a felt sense that it is safe enough for them to exist and form an energetic boundary.

Very Early On

This shows that there is far more to having boundaries than simply being able to say yes and no. It comes down to someone feeling safe enough to inhabit their body and having an energetic bubble that leads to a sense of being protected.

With this in mind, if you find it hard to stand your ground and often feel exposed, it could go back to what happened when you were an infant. The inner work that you do and even the touch that you receive are likely to help with this.

Chapter 25

Journaling

Writing about what is going on for you in a journal can also aid you on your journey of reconnecting to your true essence. Not only will you be able to track your progress, but you will be able to strengthen the connection that you have with yourself.

So, after writing in a journal for a little while, you will have the evidence in front of you of what has been going on for you and the steps you have taken. Whereas if you kept everything in, it would be a lot easier for your mind to downplay how far you have come and to forget about the small, if not the big steps, you have made.

A New Relationship

By writing down your thoughts, how you feel, and what your needs, wants, preferences and longings are, you will be acknowledging your true self. Your adult self will then be providing the acknowledgement that you missed out on during your developmental years.

In the beginning, it might be hard for you to connect to some of these inner elements, but through implementing the steps above and exploring your inner world, this will change. As to how often you use a journal, it can all depend on what is right for you.

139

A Routine

You may find that you feel the call to use one a few times a day or perhaps a few times a week. Another benefit is that, as this is your own private journal, it doesn't matter what you say or how you say it - you can freely express yourself.

If writing doesn't suit you, another option would be for you to record your thoughts. This is something you can do with your smartphone or another device you may have.

A Fresh Start

Once you have finished a journal, you may feel the need to hold onto it. This way, you will be able to look back over the months and years, as your journals accumulate and see how far you have come.

Alternatively, you may feel the need to get rid of a journal once there are no more pages left, and you can do this by burning it. While this will stop you from being able to look back over a longer period of time, it can be very liberating.

Creativity

Along with writing in a journal and writing in general, there are many things that you can do to strengthen the connection you have with yourself. Painting, acting, singing, dancing, and making things with your hands are but a few examples.

Whatever it is that you are drawn to at this time, it will allow you to express who you are. It won't be something that you do as a

k To Life

at can also assist you is to practice a martial art. This can help
u to reawaken the fire that is inside you, the fire that has been
eply repressed.

y being in an environment where it is safe for you to express this
ide of yourself in a controlled manner, you can start to connect to
key part of yourself. Finding a class where you feel comfortable
nd an instructor or instructors that you get on with will also help.

Resistance

In the beginning, you may find that it is hard for you to let yourself
go and that you are fairly restrained. This is not something that you
need to criticise yourself for.

If you have been out of touch with this side of you for a long time, it
is to be expected that it would take time. Be patient with yourself
and allow yourself to slowly reconnect with this side of yourself.

---

means to an end, something that can be an expression of your
false self; it will be something that you do as an end per se.

Travel

Visiting new places and new countries by yourself is another great
way for you to reconnect with yourself. What this can also do is
allow you to connect to parts of yourself that you didn't even know
existed.

So, if you feel the call to go somewhere and end up going there,
this will be a time when you will be meeting a number of your
needs and as you will be somewhere different, it will be up to you
to decide where you will go, what you will do, assert yourself and
ask for things.

Self-Leadership

As you won't be with anyone else, you will have to activate
yourself. In the beginning, you might feel anxious and confused,
but over time, this will change.

Leading yourself and no longer following others or waiting to be
told what to do will slowly be something that feels right. You will go
from being a passenger in someone else's car to being the driver
of your own car.

Chapter 26

Self-Activation

When it comes to activating yourself, this will be a t... will feel the call to do something and do it. You are t... to do something because you want to please anoth... because you have been told to do it.

This will show that you are not only in tune with your ... that you are also connected to your fight instinct/aggressi... it comes to the latter, this part of you will be there to pro... and it will give you the energy that you need to express you...

A Gradual Process

Being fully connected to this part of you is likely to take time... this is because it relates to you being connected to your body... by disconnecting from your body, you would have also lost to... with this part of yourself.

It is then not that this part of you is separate and can be put to on... side whilst you stay fully connected to your body; when you... connection with your body was weakened, you would have lost... touch with your aggression. Still, by working through your pain and... arousal, and questioning what you believe about your aggression,... irrespective of what this connection is currently like, this will... gradually change.

means to an end, something that can be an expression of your false self; it will be something that you do as an end per se.

Travel

Visiting new places and new countries by yourself is another great way for you to reconnect with yourself. What this can also do is allow you to connect to parts of yourself that you didn't even know existed.

So, if you feel the call to go somewhere and end up going there, this will be a time when you will be meeting a number of your needs and as you will be somewhere different, it will be up to you to decide where you will go, what you will do, assert yourself and ask for things.

Self-Leadership

As you won't be with anyone else, you will have to activate yourself. In the beginning, you might feel anxious and confused, but over time, this will change.

Leading yourself and no longer following others or waiting to be told what to do will slowly be something that feels right. You will go from being a passenger in someone else's car to being the driver of your own car.

Chapter 26

Self-Activation

When it comes to activating yourself, this will be a time when you will feel the call to do something and do it. You are then not going to do something because you want to please another person or because you have been told to do it.

This will show that you are not only in tune with your needs, but that you are also connected to your fight instinct/aggression. When it comes to the latter, this part of you will be there to protect you, and it will give you the energy that you need to express yourself.

A Gradual Process

Being fully connected to this part of you is likely to take time, and this is because it relates to you being connected to your body. So, by disconnecting from your body, you would have also lost touch with this part of yourself.

It is then not that this part of you is separate and can be put to one side whilst you stay fully connected to your body; when your connection with your body was weakened, you would have lost touch with your aggression. Still, by working through your pain and arousal, and questioning what you believe about your aggression, irrespective of what this connection is currently like, this will gradually change.

143

Back To Life

What can also assist you is to practice a martial art. This can help you to reawaken the fire that is inside you, the fire that has been deeply repressed.

By being in an environment where it is safe for you to express this side of yourself in a controlled manner, you can start to connect to a key part of yourself. Finding a class where you feel comfortable and an instructor or instructors that you get on with will also help.

Resistance

In the beginning, you may find that it is hard for you to let yourself go and that you are fairly restrained. This is not something that you need to criticise yourself for.

If you have been out of touch with this side of you for a long time, it is to be expected that it would take time. Be patient with yourself and allow yourself to slowly reconnect with this side of yourself.

Chapter 27

Two Common Sayings

Over the years, you may have heard that life is not about finding oneself, but it is about creating oneself. When you are exploring new places, this can be seen as an example of the latter.

However, as your true self is found within and not without, purely 'creating yourself' without 'finding yourself' would simply cause you to replace one false self with another false self. If you were born as an empty vessel and both a self and a purpose had to be programmed into you by society, this wouldn't be the case.

Another One

You may have also heard that you just need to 'be yourself'. But, if you are in a disconnected and repressed state and are out of touch with your true self, you won't be able to just be yourself.

Of course, as you have invested in this book, part of you wants this to change, but that doesn't mean that you can simply will yourself into letting go of your false self. This whole outlook can be seen as another consequence of the view that someone begins and ends with their conscious mind – that's all they are – and that there is no such thing as defences; defences that estrange them from their essence.

Chapter 28

What Did You Lose?

Throughout your developmental years, you might have had to lose parts of your personality and some of your interests to be accepted. This is then another way in which you lost touch with your true self.

For example, perhaps you were seen as being too sensitive or too loud and had to become tougher or quieter. You might have wanted to do something that wasn't seen as something that a boy/girl should do, and had to suppress a want that you had to try something.

Not Acceptable

You might have grown up in a family where it wasn't acceptable to be angry, and/or sad/happy. If you expressed anger and/or sadness/happiness, you might have soon been 'disciplined' in some way or isolated from others.

This could show that your parent or parents' didn't have a healthy relationship with their own anger and/or sadness/happiness. Consequently, you had to renounce parts of yourself to be accepted, and this is now stopping you from being able to be a whole human being.

An Analogy

One way to look at this would be to say that when you were younger, you were only allowed to use certain tools. Now, only

147

being able to use certain tools allowed you to survive in your early environment.

But, now that you are an adult, only being able to use certain tools will hold you back. For you to thrive, you will need to have access to all of the tools that are available and feel comfortable using them.

Something to explore

To help you find out what it is that you had to lose, simply ask yourself: what parts of myself, interests and feelings did I have to disown? By planting these seeds in your mind, you are likely to find that you start to receive answers automatically as time goes by.

Writing this question in your journal and allowing yourself to freely write whatever comes to mind will also help. You might be surprised by what you had to lose touch with.

Resistance

When you connect to a part of you, a feeling or an interest that you had to lose touch with, you could end up feeling guilty and ashamed of it. Expressing this part of you or a feeling or embracing an interest can be seen as something that will stop you from being accepted and love to be withdrawn.

This will be how it was for you very early on, and not how it has to be for you now. You can now embrace all of yourself and be accepted and loved.

Chapter 29

Inner Conflict

At times, you may experience a fair amount of resistance when it comes to expressing your needs. If so, you will see that connecting to your needs is one thing, and it is another thing altogether to feel comfortable enough to express them, or at least some of them.

What this can illustrate is that, very early on, thanks to how deprived you were, a big part of you ended up resenting having needs and came to see them as a threat to your survival. Therefore, to this part of you, expressing your needs won't merely cause you to experience pain, it will also be seen as something that will cause you to be rejected and abandoned and even ostracised and for your life to come to an end.

Inner Disharmony

This part of you, a part that will be a part of your false self, is then going to do what it can to make sure that the part of you that wants to express itself is kept under control. But, as expressing your needs is seen as something that will cause you to suffer and put your very survival at risk, it is not going to do this to harm you.

Based on the associations that were formed very early on, this will be seen as your only option, and this may mean that a big part of you feels comfortable being super independent and finds it hard to accept that you need others. Even so, this part of you will typically outmuscle the part of you that wants to connect to others, making it hard for you to be a balanced human being.

149

Another Aspect

What this or another part of you can also outmuscle are the sides of you that were not seen as being acceptable. So, it can stop you from expressing your sensitivity or the extroverted side of your nature and your anger and/or sadness/happiness, as I mentioned earlier.

If you spend a lot of time in doing mode and very little in being mode, this can also be why. Your need to relax, experience pleasure, and have fun is then going to be kept at bay.

Stay with it

Anyhow, very early on, you were a dependent human being, and now you will be an interdependent human being. There was nothing wrong with your needs at this stage of your life, and there is nothing wrong with them now - having needs is part of the human experience.

By questioning what you believe about your needs and working through the pain that is inside you (you may come into contact with anger, rage, hate, frustration, shame, hopelessness, helplessness, sadness, and hurt, with this being how you felt when your needs were not met very early on), you will gradually feel comfortable being in touch with your needs and expressing them. This doesn't mean that your needs will always be met, but it is unlikely that you will die for expressing them or be overwhelmed with pain if they are not met.

Chapter 30

Unhealthy Guilt

If you find that you struggle with feeling guilty when it comes to expressing yourself and living your own life, it will be important for you to look into why this is. When you feel guilty, it can be as though this proves that what you are doing is wrong or bad.

In reality, it can show that what you are doing simply goes against the values that were instilled into you by your parent or parents' and other authority figures that were around during your early years. Feeling guilty will then show that you are going against how another person or people wanted you to behave in order to meet their needs and doesn't actually mean that you are doing something that is inherently wrong or bad.

Drawing the Line

To be able to express yourself and live your own life without feeling guilty, it will be vital for you to question these values. The emotional work that you do will also help with this.

As you bring each value to the light, you can decide if it is a value that you agree with and is right for you. If it isn't, you can find a value that you do agree with and that is right for you.

A Few Examples

What you may find is that your family instilled the following values into you: being right, looking good, and pleasing others. The next step will be for you to see if these values are truly serving you.

151

You may soon see how each of these values is holding you back and stopping you from growing. The first can be replaced with a value that allows you to be wrong; the second with a value that allows you to make mistakes; and the third with a value that allows you to prioritise your own needs.

The Individuation process

By exploring what does and doesn't belong to you, you are letting go of what was passed onto you that has absolutely no relevance to who you are. This is likely to be something that you will do for the rest of your life, but this is simply part of owning yourself.

It is likely that you were brought up by people who hadn't taken the time to really question whether the values and beliefs that were passed onto them were right for them. Consequently, they would have had their own vehicle, so to speak, but they would have followed a path that was already laid out.

Chapter 31

Forgiveness

Based on the title of this chapter, you might have assumed that I'm going to talk about the importance of forgiving others and what you can do to gradually achieve this aim. However, although this is important, what is more important is self-forgiveness.

Upon hearing this, you might wonder what it is that you need to forgive yourself for. After all, if you were abused and neglected by one or both of your parents' and/or other family members and authority figures, you won't have done anything wrong.

A Strong Reaction

Hearing this might even make you feel angry and as though you are being blamed for what you went through. Yet, the reason why forgiving yourself is important is not that you were at fault; no, it is because you would have personalised what took place and believed you were at fault for what happened.

By believing that if you were different and behaved differently, it would have weighed you down. The outcome of this is that you are likely to have experienced a lot of self-hate, shame, guilt, and a deep sense of being unworthy and unlovable.

The Truth

Despite the meaning that an underdeveloped version of you made and how you felt by not receiving the love that you needed, how you were treated was not your fault. Knowing this, deep down, will take time.

Working through your pain and questioning what you believe will help with this. In fact, forgiving yourself can be seen as something that is largely an outgrowth of working through your emotional wounds and questioning the beliefs that you formed all those years ago.

An Exercise

Together with this, you can imagine that you are able to go back in time and meet the child that you once were. This child feels responsible for how they are being treated.

Before long, you are likely to feel a deep sense of compassion for this child. There will be no doubt in your mind that this child is not responsible for the harm that they are experiencing.

Breaking Through

This technique won't necessarily heal anything for you at an emotional level, but what it is likely to do is play a part in changing how you perceive what you went through and start to break down the walls that make it hard for you to let good into your life. What this will do is make it easier for you to let go of your need to blame yourself.

And, as what you went through wasn't your fault, it means that you deserve to be here, to exist, to experience joy, be supported, loved, and valued. A big part of you might reject this right now, but that doesn't change this fact.

The Other Side

To take a step back now and return to the other type of forgiveness, forgiving those that have hurt you, and assuming it was your parents, perhaps you have been told that you just need to forgive your parent or parents' and even to 'get over' what happened. The main reason that could be put forward for the first part is that they did the best that they could.

Due to this, it will be as though they don't need to be held accountable for their behaviour. Unlike when an adult harms another adult, then, they will be held to different standards.

Less-Than

This whole outlook can be seen as a consequence of how a child is often seen as having less value than an adult. Unlike an adult, they are not entitled to be treated with the same level of respect, have the same rights, or be worthy of being seen and heard.

Most likely, they did do the best that they could, but this won't have changed the fact that they caused you a lot of harm. If you were to go back in time and tell the child you once were that their parents are doing the best they can, would it change anything? It's unlikely.

A Natural Outcome

The general view that it's simply about forgiving and then moving on not only completely bypasses the emotional impact of what took place, but it also doesn't acknowledge that there is emotional work to be done. It's a view that can easily be both held and expressed by someone who was perhaps also mistreated but is too out of touch with themselves to realise this.

This type of forgiveness then becomes another way for them to please and protect their parents and keep their own unhealed wounds at bay. And, in a society with numerous other individuals who are in the same position, it can lead to a lot of approval.

The Other Piece

If you have been told, at least once, that you need to 'get over' what happened, you may have also heard that 'life is too short' to hold onto resentment, anger, and/or hate, for instance. And how this is not harming anyone else; it is only harming you.

You might then have felt bad about not being able to simply let go and move on with your life. These phrases can be seen as yet another consequence of living in a mind-centric society, and how letting go is seen as something that takes place through force.

Denial

If this doesn't happen, it is then a sign that you haven't tried hard enough or don't actually want to move on from what happened. But, even if you solely focused on letting go mentally and not emotionally, you are unlikely to have actually forgiven anyone.

What you are likely to find is that you have just suppressed how you really feel due to feeling guilty and ashamed, and out of the need to please another or others. Quite simply, thanks to your brain's ability to remove material from your conscious awareness, deceiving yourself into believing you have moved on is one thing; it is another thing altogether to have emotionally moved on.

The Main Purpose

This comes back to what I said earlier about how your brain is designed to keep you unconscious. And, how it does this so that you can keep it together and function, and, thereby, pass on your genes.

The fact that you are committed to becoming a more integrated human being shows that there is a part of you that wants to embrace what is actually going on for you; you don't want to live a lie. This is something that takes courage and is perhaps a consequence of you having come to see that you have no other option than to face yourself.

No Different

So, just as forgiving yourself is likely to be an outgrowth of you working through your pain, so is forgiving others. By engaging in this process, you might soon find that it gets easier for you to see your parent or parents', and others more clearly and accept them as they are without trying to change them or receive anything from them.

You would then have seen them as all-powerful and all-knowing gods when you were growing up, but it will become clear that they were just wounded human beings who were also likely to have been deprived of what they needed during their formative years (and perhaps this is something that goes back many, many generations). How they treated you was then a reflection of what was going on for them, not a reflection of how worthy and lovable you were.

Chapter 32

Supportive Relationships

You might be in a position where you have one or a number of friends with who you are able to be yourself around. Or, you might not have anyone in your life that you can be your real self around.

Even if you only have one person like this in your life, their presence and support will make a massive difference. If you don't have anyone in your life like this right now, keep in mind that this is just a stage that you are passing through.

A Transitional Period

As for the people in your life who reflect your false self, these people are likely to fall away as time goes by. Spending time with people who you are unable to be yourself around simply won't interest you.

You may also find that some of your existing relationships change, and you grow closer to certain people. What you can keep in mind is that you will meet the people you need to meet when you need to meet them.

Building Connections

There are, of course, certain places you can go to where you may meet people who are on the path, and you could end up becoming close friends with them. For example, you could go on a course, join a support group or attend an event.

At the same time, you could meet someone on a bus, train, or when you are out walking, with who you could become close friends. One part will be doing the inner work, and the other part will be putting yourself out there when you feel the call to do so.

Chapter 33

The Power Of Visualisation

When it comes to working through inner wounds, you may believe that once this is done, it will be possible for you to live a fulfilling life. Until that point, your life can end up being put on hold in many ways.

What I have come to believe is that this is unlikely to be something that will ever be achieved, and it doesn't need to be achieved to be able to live a fulfilling life. However, if you are not in a good way, it can take time for you to find your feet and truly embrace life.

Two Components

With this in mind, I believe that in addition to you doing the inner work and doing certain things, it is also important to use the power of your mind to allow you to live a fulfilling life. Earlier on, when I mentioned the law of resonance, I said that your thoughts, emotions, feelings, beliefs, and trauma have an effect on what you do and don't experience.

What this means is that you can use your thoughts, emotions, and feelings to allow you to experience something. To do this, you will need to imagine that you are already experiencing that which you want to experience and feel the feelings and think the thoughts that you would have.

One Moment

As to why you would imagine that you have what you desire, now it's because there is only now. Time exists on one level, but at a deeper level, there is no time or space.

And, while your thoughts will play a part in you having certain feelings, it is your feelings that have the real power. Another part of this will involve you taking inspired action.

Putting it all together

So, let's pretend that you wanted to manifest a friend who is on the path and is supportive, empathetic, and compassionate. To do this, you can sit down somewhere, start playing some music that elates your mood, and then close your eyes.

You can then imagine that you are sitting in front of this friend, having a drink and/or something to eat. You can use your thoughts to allow yourself to feel supported, valued, and at ease, for instance.

All your senses

To make this even more real, you can go into what it would smell like, what you would hear, how your body feels in the chair and the taste that is in your mouth. This is something that you can do for a few minutes each day or a few times a week.

After a while, you might experience the urge to do something or go somewhere. This will be an example of inspired action, as you won't be forcing yourself to do something.

A Hurdle

The other part of this is not being attached to a certain outcome and trusting in the process. If you are strongly attached to an outcome, you will be coming from a place of not having what you desire, and so you will experience more of the same.

Also, you have to embody the vibrational frequency of what you want to experience for there to be a match and to pull it toward you. This is why not being in the right place internally will repel what you want; it will be as though what you want is on another planet and is completely out of your reach.

Less-Effort

Not feeling worthy or safe enough to have what you desire, or questioning if it is even possible, can also push what you desire away. From this, what may be clear is that it will get easier for you to experience things as you work through the layers of pain inside you and settle down, and what might also stand out is how important it is for you to question what you believe is possible.

And, as you become more whole and integrated, there will be less conflict inside you, and you will be more in alignment with what you want, and thereby, your life will be more streamlined. What this emphasises is how it is the parts of yourself that get in the way (and create external hurdles), and as these parts merge with the rest of you, your life can flow.

Chapter 34

The Power Of Your Environment

In the last chapter, I said that you might believe that once you have worked through all of your inner wounds, you will be able to live a fulfilling life. This will then be a point when you will always be connected and able to express yourself.

I then said that this might not ever take place, and it doesn't need to take place either for you to be able to live a life that is worth living. If this is not something that you can accept right now, perhaps due to how much pain you are in and the beliefs that you have, it is likely to be something that you can accept in time.

A Big Impact

Another part of what will make it easier for you to be connected to and express who you are will be to live in an environment that is supportive. So, this will relate to where you live, the area, the people in your life, and what the climate is like.

Each of these elements, as well as others, can make it easier or harder for you to be yourself. Not unexpectedly, if so many of these elements in your life are not supportive of who you are, a lot of your energy is going to be spent resisting what is going on around you.

It might not stand out

But, if, for example, you have always lived in a certain way, you might not be aware of what kind of environment is right for you or what it is in your current environment that is undermining you. Like a fish that has always lived in dirty water, this will just be what is normal.

If the fish were asked what it is like living in dirty water, it wouldn't understand what is being said. Nonetheless, if the fish were put in clean water, it would soon get a sense of how bleak it was before, but only thanks to the fact that it now has a new reference point with which it can compare its old environment.

A Hypothetical Scenario

For a moment, imagine that you live in a busy city (perhaps you do) and you always have, you have never left this city and experienced what it is like to live in the country. Furthermore, where you live is usually cold, you have had the same friends since you were at school, and the average person is consumed by stress.

You are then doing the inner work, but you feel, now and then, that something else is missing. But, as this is all you have known, you are unable to put your finger on what that is.

The Next Phase

You then continue to do the inner work and do the best you can to keep your head up and out of the blue, an opportunity comes along for you to visit another country. At first, you are not sure about whether you want to go as part of you feels comfortable where you are, but as you know that something is not right, you go for it anyway.

Once you arrive, it doesn't take long for you to notice that there are not many people around, it is warm, and the average person appears to be more laid back. You will still be on planet Earth, but it might seem as though you have been transported to another planet.

A Better Fit

What these and other elements will then do is make it easier for you to be in touch with and express yourself. Now that you have experienced something different, the reason why your other environment wasn't right will have started to stand out.

If it wasn't for this change, you would have continued to have this sense that something wasn't right, but that would have been as far as it went. Now that you are somewhere else entirely, you will have a new reference point; your world will have expanded, and you will know that there is somewhere that is right for you, or, at the very least, a better fit.

The Central Point

This is why it has been said that we don't know what we don't know. By having new experiences and trying things that you haven't tried before, you will get a better sense of what is, and what isn't, right for you.

For you to be in an environment that is right for you, it might not be as extreme as moving to another country. But, even if this is something that you feel the call to do, it could still take time for this to happen.

Baby Steps

In the short-term, it could merely be a case of you spending time in nature or by the sea and joining a few social clubs, for instance. You will then have the same home and live in the same area, but what you do will strengthen you, preparing you to take bigger steps.

If where you live is not right for you and you have the need to move somewhere else, but you don't have the means to do so at this time, it would be easy for you to feel overwhelmed and helpless. It would be such a huge jump that it would seem to be out of your reach.

What can you do?

By focusing on the steps that you can take to make it easier for you to be connected and express yourself, you won't be consumed by what is currently out of your reach. As Desmond Tutu once said, "There is only one way to eat an elephant: a bite at a time."

To send this point home, when you next look at a massive building, keep in mind that it didn't just appear overnight; it took a lot of building materials and many hours of labour to build. The people who built it did what they could when they could, and this allowed them to gradually put together what you can now see with your own eyes.

Not an Island

This all comes down to the fact that you are an independent human being who is on a journey. You are then no different from a tree or a plant, insofar as you need the right conditions to be able to thrive and time to grow into who you were born to be.

And, as you develop a better connection to your body and your feelings and needs, it will get easier for you to take inspired action. You can then feel the urge to do something, and you will do it.

Chapter 35

Are You Following Your Calling?

Another part of what will make up your environment is where you go to work. And, even if you work remotely or are self-employed, what you do will still impact you.

What will be different is that if you work around others, you might have less control over your environment. Whereas if you can work wherever you desire or from home, you will have greater control over your environment,

A Number of Scenarios

When it comes to what you do for a living, this might be something that allows you to stay connected to and express your true self. At the same time, it could be something that doesn't.

Or, there could be certain parts of what you do that are in alignment with your true self and parts that aren't. Either way, if you spend a lot of time working, what you do is going to have a big impact on your life.

One Example

Let's pretend, for a moment, that you are a nurse and that you love what you do. It allows you to be of service and to make a difference to the lives of others.

Nonetheless, while you love what you do, you often feel exhausted as you work too many hours and overlook a number of your own needs. How you behave in this area of your life can then be seen as being influenced by both your true self and your false self.

A Blend of the Two

Being of service and making a difference will reflect your true self, and not being able to be there for yourself will be a reflection of your false self. Deep down, you can believe that if you were to express your needs and make it clear that you can no longer work as much, your survival would be put under threat.

You will then be abandoning yourself, as this will be seen as your only way to survive. In this case, as you gradually phase out your false self, you could end up working fewer hours at the same organisation or even work for a different organisation.

Another Example

Or, you could end up finding that what you do is not something that is in alignment with your true self. So, while you will want to be of service and make a difference, being a nurse is not something that you feel called to do.

What you could end up finding out is that what led you down this path is that you had to be there for one of your parents and/or a sibling. This is what allowed you to be accepted and approved of.

A Different Direction

As the connection with yourself builds and you feel more comfortable expressing yourself, you could end up doing something completely different. You are likely to still do something that allows you to be of service and make a difference, but it will be more in alignment with who you are.

Perhaps you are, or aren't, a nurse, and perhaps you do, or don't, enjoy being one, but you could be in a position where you want to make a few adjustments to what you do or to change what you do.

As with changing other parts of your environment, focusing on taking one step at a time is important to prevent you from feeling overwhelmed and helpless.

A Helping Hand

What can help you to gain a clearer understanding of what is right for you is to ask yourself a number of questions. The first is: what would you do if you didn't care about what anyone else thought?

The second is: what would you do if you only had a few years to live? The third is: what would you do if money were no longer something you needed?

Chapter 36

Energy

As you may already know, it takes a lot of energy to break through defences and work through pain. It is for this reason that it is important for you to consume the right nutrients, exercise, and have enough sleep (the supportive relationships you have or will have are also part of what will energise you).

This will give you strength and make it easier for you to keep going. There is a lot of information online about optimising each of these areas, but I will touch upon some of the basics.

Nutrition

It goes without saying that it is important to eat right, and there are supplements that can be helpful too. Supplements are often seen as a waste of money, but the nutritional content of food today is not what it once was (also, stress is said to deplete certain vitamins and minerals, so if you feel stressed, you might need more than usual).

When it comes to supplements, some of the main ones are: magnesium (and there are many types, so it will be a good idea for you to find the one that is right for you), B vitamins, omega-3 fatty acids, and vitamin C. There are also adaptogens – these are made from plants and mushrooms – that can help you to feel more relaxed and improve your overall wellbeing.

Two Brains

Not only do you have a brain in your head, but you also have one in your stomach. This other brain has been described as the enteric nervous system, and it has been said that over 90 per cent of serotonin and over 50 per cent of dopamine are created there.

Looking after your other brain is then going to be vital. Part of what is likely to allow this brain to function at its best will be for you to consume probiotics such as kefir, kimchi, and sauerkraut.

Digestive Issues

Having said that, you may find that your stomach tightens up at certain times, and this makes it difficult for this part of you to function at its best. When this happens, it might not matter what probiotics you consume.

As your stomach is where your third chakra is located and is the area of your personal power, it can tighten up when you feel as though you have no control and don't feel safe enough (first chakra) to assert yourself. Considering this, the inner work that you do will play a part in your stomach being able to function properly.

Exercise

Thankfully, there are many ways for you to look after your physical health. You might not enjoy running, but what you could do is walk, cycle or swim on a regular basis.

Lifting weights has numerous benefits, such as improving bone health, brain health, and mood. Yet, if lifting weights is not something that interests you, you can do bodyweight exercises instead.

Sleep

It has been said that, when it comes to sleep, it is best to have a consistent sleep schedule. This involves both going to bed and waking up at the same time, and having around eight hours of sleep.

To help you fall asleep at night, if this is an issue, you can listen to relaxing music, read a book that is not going to unsettle you, and make sure that you are not exposed to blue light a few hours before. Your smartphone (and other devices you may have) emits blue light, and this suppresses melatonin, a hormone that makes you sleepy.

Chapter 37

The Power Of Your Attention

You may have heard sayings such as what you focus on grows and where your mind goes is where your energy flows. What this illustrates is how powerful your attention is.

If, on the other hand, you could direct your attention to something and nothing happened, it wouldn't matter what you focused on. However, by playing a role and having the need to please others, for a long time, your energy will have been directed towards others, causing you to deprive yourself in the process.

Another Element

On one side, your life will have been deprived, and on the other, by being outer-directed, you would have deprived your own being. Meditating and/or being in nature, the inner work that you do and Yoga, Tai Chi or Chi Gong will allow you to gradually bring more of your attention towards yourself.

Another thing that you can do is to consciously direct your attention to different parts of your body and bring your energy towards yourself. And, if you have spent a lot of time living in your head, your body is likely to have spent a lot of time without much attention.

One option

As with meditating, first, you can find somewhere that is quiet and where you can sit with your back upright. Second, you can bring your attention down to your feet and work your way up to your head.

You can focus on each body part for a few seconds, or you could set a timer so each body part receives a certain amount of your attention. This can be a time when you experience a deep sense of love and appreciation for each body part.

Another Option

Alternatively, instead of focusing on each body part, you can focus on different parts of your body. One way you can do this is to focus on your base chakra first and move your attention through each chakra and end at your crown chakra.

In case you don't know what a 'chakra' is, it is an energy centre in your body, and each centre corresponds to a different area of your life. Furthermore, each one has a different colour, and the fourth one is the bridge between the lower physical ones and the upper spiritual ones.

A Short Description

This brief explanation will not only allow you to gain a deeper understanding of each chakra, but it will also help you to develop better emotional literacy. That is to say, if you experience a sensation in a certain part of your body and are unable to describe how you feel or the feelings you are experiencing, this will assist you.

The first chakra is located at the base of your spine, is red, and relates to the area of survival, so security, stability, support, trust, and safety. Fear and terror are also associated with this one.

The second chakra is located in your sacral area, is orange, and relates to sexuality, pleasure, and creativity. The main feeling associated with this one is guilt.

The third chakra is located in your solar plexus, is yellow, and relates to personal power and self-confidence. Some of the feelings associated with this one are anger, rage, shame, and power.

The fourth chakra is located in your chest, is green, and relates to love and connection. Some of the feelings associated with this one are love, loss, grief, and sadness.

The fifth chakra is located in your throat, is blue, and is associated with self-expression and communication. Although this is not really an area where feelings are experienced, it is an area where there can be a sense of tension if there is a blockage, or ease when there isn't.

The sixth chakra is located in the centre of your forehead, is indigo, and relates to being able to see clearly. Once again, while this is not really an area where feelings are experienced, it can lead to a sense of confusion when it is not functioning as it should and clarity when it is.

The seventh chakra is located at the top of your head, is purple, and relates to your connection to the universe. As with the previous two, this is not really associated with feelings, and when this centre is not functioning as it should, it can lead to a sense of being disconnected, and when it is, a sense of being connected.

The Next Step

With this understanding in place, you can bring your attention down to your lower hips and imagine feeling safe and supported. You can then imagine that you are slowly moving the colour red up to the top of your head and then down again, and do this for as long as your desire.

You can bring this energy up to your head with your in-breath and down with your out-breath and so on and so forth. You are then cycling this energy through your body.

The Same Process

After you have finished moving this energy around, you can move on to the next chakra and go through the same process until you have focused on each one. If you stick to this process, you might end up being surprised by the impact that this activity has on your life.

This is a time when you are not trying to change how you feel and engaging in suppression; you are merely exercising your imagination. However, if this is not something that feels comfortable at this time, you can simply put it to one side, and perhaps, try it at another stage of your journey.

Chapter 38

Emotional Awareness

As well as looking into the chakra system to gain a better understanding of how you feel, you can also explore the findings of a Finnish study on the bodily location of emotion. For the time being, the list below will assist you with this.

In Alphabetical Order

Anger – this is likely to be experienced in your hands, arms, and shoulders, just above your stomach, and in your mouth and face.

Anxiety – this is likely to be experienced in your face, neck, chest, just above your stomach, and throughout your legs and feet.

Fear – this is likely to be experienced throughout your whole body.

Guilt – this is likely to be experienced in your stomach and face. Additionally, this feeling can make you feel as though you have done something bad.

Helpless – this is likely to be experienced just above your stomach and in your chest. Also, this can be something that permeates your whole being with you being in a state of helplessness - it is then not that you feel helpless; it will be that you are helpless.

Hopeless – this is likely to be experienced in your chest.

Powerless – this is likely to be experienced just above your stomach.

Rage – just like anger, this is likely to be experienced in your hands, arms, and shoulders, just above your stomach, and in your mouth and face.

Sadness – this is likely to be experienced in your chest, neck, and face.

Shame – this is likely to be experienced just above your stomach, chest, shoulders, neck, and face. Additionally, this feeling can make you feel that you are bad and make you feel that you need to hide.

Also, in the same way that you can be in a state of helplessness, you can be in a state of shame where it has permeated your whole being. In both cases, this will show that your parasympathetic nervous system has been activated.

Worthless – this is likely to be experienced just above your stomach and in your face.

Chapter 39

A Useful System

Lastly, I don't think it would be right for me not to talk about something called Human Design when it comes to being in touch with and expressing your true self. There are many options available when it comes to aiding in self-understanding, such as Astrology, Numerology, The Enneagram, Cards of Destiny, and The Secret Language of Birthdays.

What Human Design will do is allow you to gain a deeper understanding of yourself, what your strengths are, and what you need to do to live a fulfilling life. This is a system that combines the I Ching, Astrology, Vedic philosophy, and Kabbalah.

The Next Step

If this is something that interests you, you can find a website online that will allow you to create a free chart. To do this, you will need your date of birth, time of birth, and place of birth.

Once you see your details appear, you can take a look at what each element means. There is a lot to learn, as you may soon realise.

A Recommendation

One book I have found to be beneficial is *"Human Design: Discover the Person You Were Born to Be"* by Chetan Parkyn. Not every element from your chart is explored in this book, but many parts are.

Afterword

As this is a process, it is imperative that you keep going and don't give up even if you feel stuck or as though your life is not changing. At the same time, even if you do have moments when you give up, there is no need for you to beat yourself up, and it doesn't mean you are a failure.

During this time, and at any other time for that matter, you can be kind and compassionate towards yourself. If you find that it is often difficult for you to be this way, the work that you do on yourself will allow you to phase out your inner critic (the part of you that can appear to be your conscience) and develop self-love.

Another way of looking at this would be to say that the work that you do on yourself will allow you to develop a loving inner mother and a supportive inner father. The former will nourish you and the latter will imbue you with courage.

In the meantime, there are a number of things that you can do. First, when you are being hard on yourself, you can imagine that a supportive friend is standing in front of you and think about what they would say to you.

Second, you can imagine how you would respond if a supportive friend or even a child made a mistake; in all likelihood, you would be kind towards them. The truth is that you deserve this level of kindness.

To stay on track, keep in mind why you are doing all this work and focus on how your life will be when you have a strong connection to your body and feel safe enough to be you. Thinking about how your life will be in a few more years if it doesn't change can also help.

You are here to express who you are, not to play a role, and live a life worth living, and I believe that your reality will reflect this as long as you are courageous, patient, and persistent. Keep in mind that no matter how you experience life at this point in time, it doesn't reflect who you are.

If you have anything you would like to share with me, feel free to get in touch. So, as a fellow traveller on the path, I wish you the very best on your journey of reconnecting to and expressing your real self.

Oliver JR Cooper

Acknowledgements

When I think about the people who have played a part in me gradually being able to reveal more of my true self, a number of people come to my attention.

When my shell was cracked, so to speak, and I could no longer play a role, I ended up spending time with a friend who I had met at college a little while before. This was Adam Jordan.

There was also another friend of mine who I met at college called Brian Reynolds. The difference here was that I had been spending time with this friend ever since we met all those years ago.

I felt that I could be authentic with these two people, and there was no need for me to act strong or as though I had it all together. They were down-to-earth and real.

As time went by, I started to come into contact with other people with who I could be myself around. One of these people was Tony Stuart.

After this, I met someone called Ian Baillie. He is also very down to earth, kind, bright, and extremely generous.

A few years after this, I met someone called Wain Gordon. When I think about Wain, what comes to mind is someone who is authentic, sharp, and very accepting.

There are then, of course, the healers and therapists that I worked with throughout this time. Vijay Rana is one of those and a true expert at what he does.

There is then Ben Ralston, who is an incredibly gifted healer, and Caroline Purvey; a no-nonsense teacher who teaches TRE and yoga. And, last but not least, Oliver Tatt and Leila Maktari.